HANDCRAFTED WOODEN TOYS

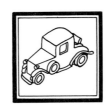

Ralph S. Buckland

5 Sterling Publishing Co., Inc.   New York

DEDICATION

To my wife Kathy and our children Jessica, Bernie, Kimberly and Jennifer.

ACKNOWLEDGMENTS

A special thanks to Dean Marple for his guidance and fine photography work inside the book.

As on previous occasions, thanks to Doug and Betty Osborn for the many times they have been willing to help with computer problems I've encountered.

Thanks to the following persons who were willing to help in various ways: Bea Barnett, Terry Adams, Jamie Fisher, Mikie and Shelly Bolte, John Patterson, Mike Cea, Karen Nelson, and Eduardo Fausti.

Popular Science Books offers a wood identification kit that includes 30 samples of cabinet woods. For details on ordering, please write: Popular Science Books, P.O. Box 2033, Latham, N.Y. 12111.

Edited by Michael Cea

Library of Congress Cataloging-in-Publication Data
Buckland, Ralph S.
    Handcrafted wooden toys.
    Includes index.
    1. Wooden toy making. I. Title.
TT174.5.W6B795 1987 745.592   86-30098
ISBN 0-8069-6456-1 (pbk.)

3   5   7   9   10   8   6   4   2

Copyright © 1987 by Ralph S. Buckland
Published by Sterling Publishing Co., Inc.
Two Park Avenue, New York, N.Y. 10016
Distributed in Canada by Oak Tree Press Ltd.
% Canadian Manda Group, P.O. Box 920, Station U
Toronto, Ontario, Canada M8Z 5P9
Distributed in the United Kingdom by Blandford Press
Link House, West Street, Poole, Dorset BH15 ILL, England
Distributed in Australia by Capricorn Ltd.
P.O. Box 665, Lane Cove, NSW 2066
Manufactured in the United States of America

Table of Contents

Toymaking Basics   5
  Mechanical drawings   6
  Tools   18
  Techniques and Tips   37
Projects   47
  Model T Sedan   48
  Pickup Truck   54
  MG (Sports Car)   60
  Model T Coupé   66
  Eighteen Wheeler   72
  Steam Shovel   84
  Crane   91
  Train   98
  Ironing Board and Iron   106
  Toaster   111
  Vacuum Cleaner   115
  Stove   119
  Sink   127
  Refrigerator and Freezer   134
  Puzzles   141
  Penny Pool   161
  Skittles   164

Biplane   *169*
Piper Cub   *176*
Helicopter   *184*
American/British Terminology   *189*
Metric Equivalency Chart   *190*
Index   *191*
Color Section opposite page *64*

TOYMAKING
BASICS

Mechanical Drawings

Man has developed two basic methods of conveying ideas and feelings through drawings. The first method consists of pictures drawn from a strictly artistic standpoint that require little need for standardization. The second method consists of formal mechanical drawings that adhere to a set of rules that are understood throughout the world. These mechanical drawings are used exclusively throughout this book.

The draftsperson may use a variety of types of mechanical drawings. To the novice, these drawings—with their unfamiliar vocabulary of lines, views, and strange symbols—may seem at first glance to be hopelessly complex and confusing. However, when they are examined more closely, a logical method of conveying ideas can be discovered. But before this can be done—and before the novice can apply these methods to making handcrafted toys—he has to understand the following basics: the different types of drawings, how to read the lines and symbols found on these drawings, how to use grids to enlarge patterns, and which tools are the proper ones to use for layout.

TYPES OF DRAWINGS

There are two general types of mechanical drawings: *pictorial* drawings (such as one-, two-, and three-point perspectives, as well as oblique, isometric, diametric, and trimetric drawings), which show the object in picture form, and *multiview* drawings, which show the object with each view drawn separately.

A pictorial drawing shows several views in one drawing (Illus. 1). These types of drawings show views similar to those one sees when looking through a camera at an object. They generally make the shape and appearance of a toy easier to understand than drawings using one, two, or three views.

The *isometric* drawing is a pictorial drawing that is used extensively throughout industry to illustrate small objects (Illus. 2). It is also used throughout this book. An isometric drawing is not used on a large object because it would make the object appear distorted since the object's lines do not vanish. (A large toy does look more realistic when the lines vanish.) However, the isometric drawing is well suited for small objects because it is not important that the lines on these objects vanish.

Since the lines remain parallel in an isometric drawing, templates (plastic sheets with cutouts of holes, nuts, bolts, etc.) can be made to conform to isometric drawings. These types of drawings allow the draftsman to work more quickly and precisely. A large selection of templates for isometric drawings are available in art stores and most business-supply stores.

An *oblique* drawing is another form of pictorial drawing (Illus. 3). Sometimes it is used in industry, but not nearly as often as

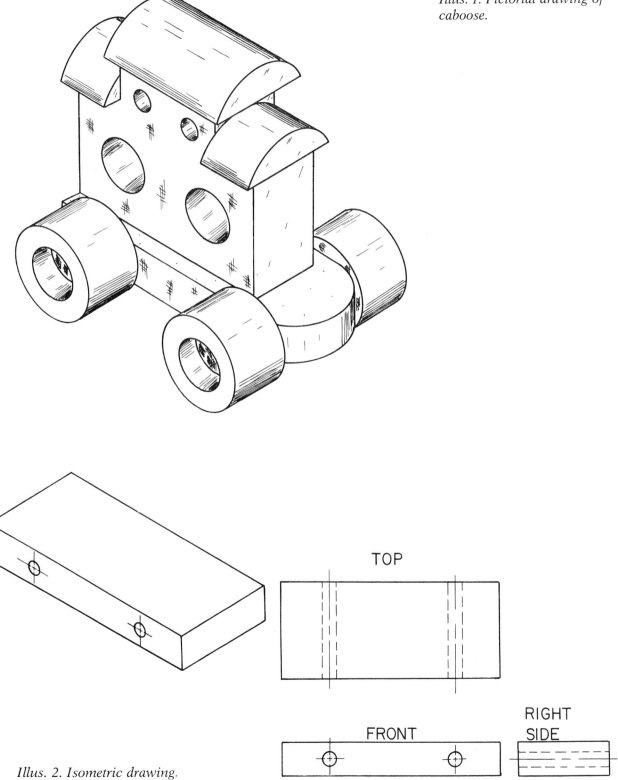

Illus. 1. Pictorial drawing of caboose.

TOP

FRONT

RIGHT
SIDE

Illus. 2. Isometric drawing.

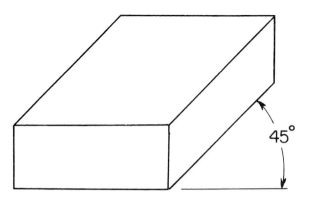

Illus. 3. Oblique drawing.

the isometric drawing. The 45° angle is commonly used in an oblique drawing, although other angles may be used.

The *one-point perspective* (Illus. 4) is used to show the inside of a room. The *two-point perspective* (Illus. 4) is used for residential home drawings. The *three-point perspective* (Illus. 5) is commonly used by architects to represent tall buildings.

A drawing showing all the necessary information to build an object (size, shape, and material) is called a *working drawing*. Working drawings are used throughout the book. So are exploded assembly drawings (Illus. 6), which show how the parts fit together.

The multiview drawing, a suitable drawing for depicting small toy parts, is also used throughout this book. The multiview drawing shows an object projected onto an imaginary plane or surface (Illus. 7). The theory behind such a drawing is that the person looking at the object can only see one side at a time, and his lines of sight are parallel. Although in reality one's lines of sight are not parallel, they do converge in a cone-like fashion towards the eyes.

Multiview drawings can have one or more views. The complexity of the object being drawn will determine the number of views needed. An example of a project needing one view is the penny pool game (Illus. 8). Its thickness can be easily stated in a note. Other views of this project are not needed, and would only be a waste of time and paper. Drawings for other toys, such as a cylinder or the smokestack on a train, may need only two views (Illus. 9): either the front or right-side view, since they reveal the same information, and the top view.

The most common type of multiview drawing, however, uses three views: the front, top, and right-side views. Only rarely are the left-side, bottom, or back view needed, because the information required to build the object is usually provided for in the three basic views (Illus. 10). There are times, however, when the shape cannot be seen using the normal multiview drawing. The *section view* shows the object as if

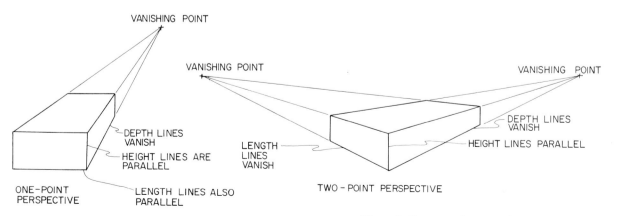

Illus. 4. One- and two-point perspectives.

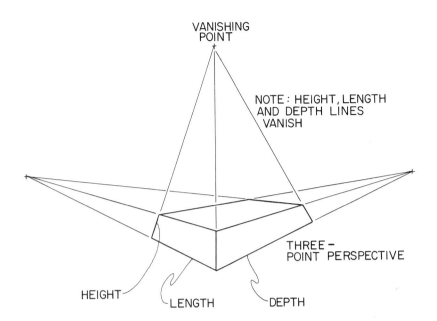

VANISHING
POINT

NOTE: HEIGHT, LENGTH
AND DEPTH LINES
VANISH

THREE -
POINT PERSPECTIVE

HEIGHT   LENGTH   DEPTH

*Illus. 5. Three-point
perspective.*

*Illus. 6. Exploded assembly
drawing of caboose.*

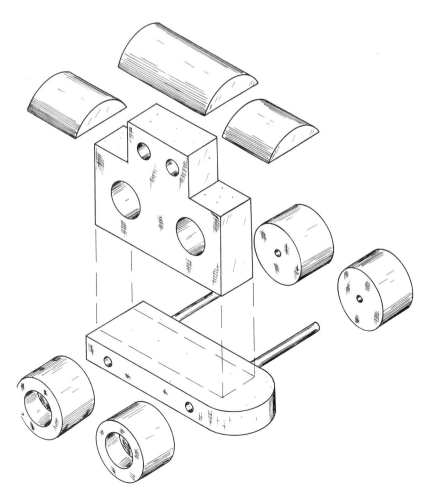

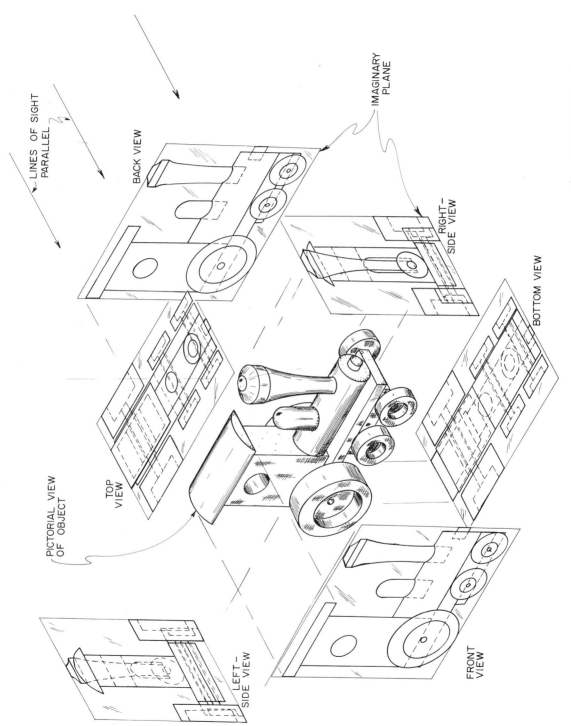

Illus. 7. Multiview drawing.

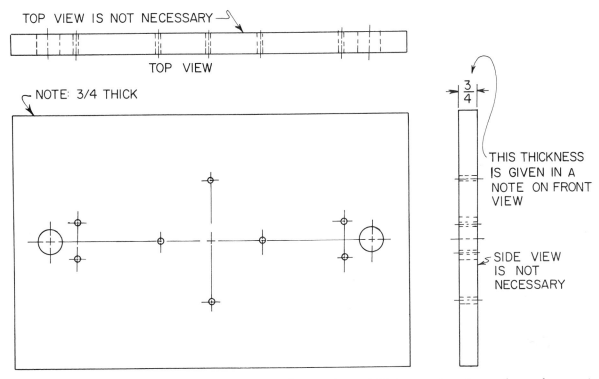

TOP VIEW IS NOT NECESSARY

TOP VIEW

NOTE: 3/4 THICK

3/4

THIS THICKNESS IS GIVEN IN A NOTE ON FRONT VIEW

SIDE VIEW IS NOT NECESSARY

Illus. 8. The penny pool game (page 161) is a project that only needs one view.

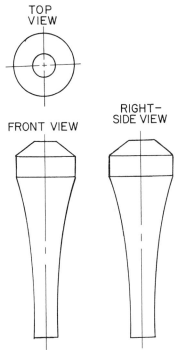

TOP VIEW

FRONT VIEW

RIGHT-SIDE VIEW

Illus. 9. The smokestack for the train (page 98) only needs two views.

it were actually cut open (Illus. 11), as though the viewer were seeing inside the shape.

A note about the drawings that appear in the project section: All dimensions given are in inches. However, to avoid cluttering up the drawings, I have not put in inch marks.

TYPES OF LINES

When mechanical drawings are used in toymaking, several types of lines are employed. These lines, often called the "alphabet of lines" (Illus. 12), tell the reader specific messages.

The *object* or *visible* line shows all the edges or corners that can actually be seen on the object.

Hidden lines are used to show the part of an object that cannot be seen. They are used on multiview drawings, but are rarely

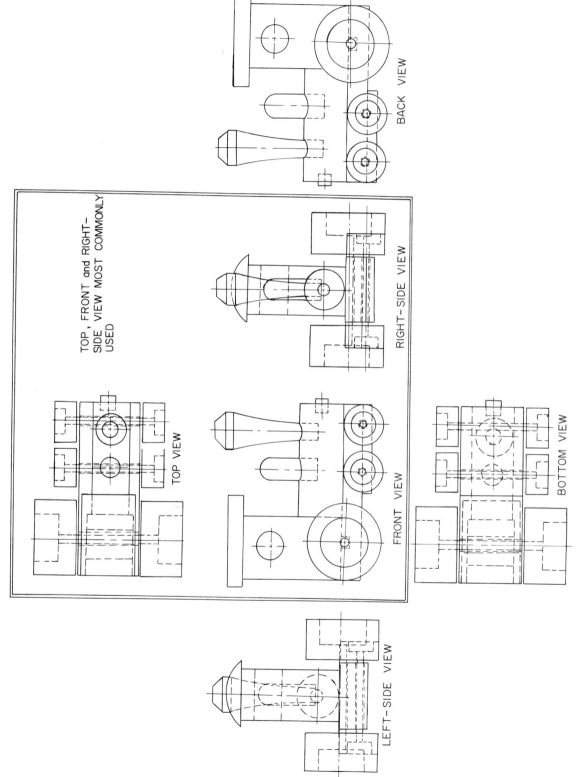

TOP, FRONT and RIGHT-SIDE VIEW MOST COMMONLY USED

BACK VIEW

RIGHT-SIDE VIEW

TOP VIEW

FRONT VIEW

BOTTOM VIEW

LEFT-SIDE VIEW

Illus. 10. Three basic views.

used on pictorial drawings. Hidden lines are depicted by a series of short dashes.

Center lines are used to show the exact center of an object or a feature of an object, such as a hole's center. Center lines are made with an alternating long and short dashed line.

Dimension lines are usually thinner than the object lines. They are used with a number to tell the size of a part. Dimension lines will usually touch an extension line, and have arrowheads that point to the exact location.

Extension lines are lines that extend from the object. They are used in conjunction with dimension lines to place sizes in an understandable location not on the object but on the outside of the object.

Section lines are easily recognized because there are usually a series of them in one spot. They also are normally drawn at a slant or angle of 30°, 45°, or 60°. Section

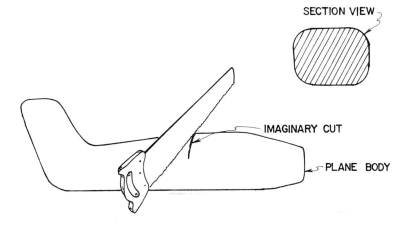

Illus. 11. Section view.

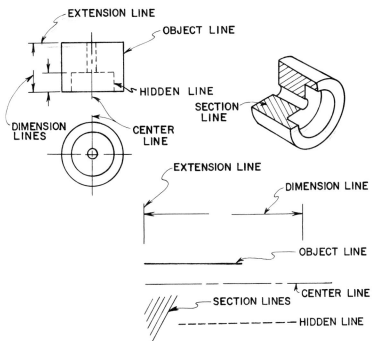

Illus. 12. "Alphabet of lines."

lines are used to show a part of the object that has been visually cut away to more clearly show the reader the part's shape.

SYMBOLS

When a mechanical drawing is read, several symbols can be frequently seen (Illus. 13). The symbol CL, usually made with the letters together, is used to locate the main center of an object. The draftsperson will often design a fancy CL, thus improving the overall appearance of a drawing.

The symbols R and DIA. are both used when circles and arcs, such as holes and round corners, are given dimensions. DIA. is an abbreviation for diameter. The diameter of a circle is the distance from one side to the other side through the center in a straight line; this is the longest path. The sizes of drills are stated in diameters; for example, a 1-inch drill is stated as a 1″ diameter hole.

The symbol R is used to give a radius dimension. The radius is the distance from the center of a circle to the edge. The R symbol is mostly used by the draftsperson to give a dimension to an arc or part of a circle, as opposed to the entire circle.

The degree symbol is a small circle placed at the right-hand side and near the top of a number. It is used to tell the number of degrees in an angle or circle.

GRIDS

Grids (Illus. 14) are used throughout the book as an easy method to enlarge a pattern. Many times, especially where irregular curves are used, it is much easier to convey the shape of an object with a grid instead of multiview or isometric drawings that use dimensions.

To copy and enlarge designs from the grids in the book, do the following: On a

Illus. 13. Symbols.

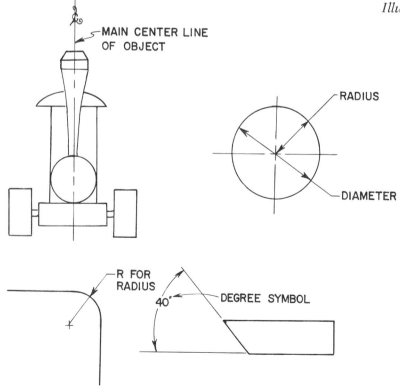

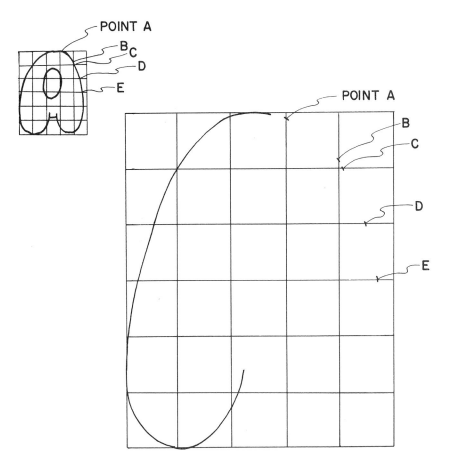

Illus. 14. Grid.

sheet of paper about the size that you want the project to be, divide the space up with exactly the same number of squares as occupied by the design in the book. The size of the larger set of squares can be determined by the enlargement ratio desired. If you want the design twice the size, then draw squares twice as big as those on the grid in the book.

Now, copy the design in the book onto the sheet of paper, square by square. Copy each point of the original pattern onto the graph squares. Curves may be drawn by eye after locating them with reference to their surrounding square. However, it is more accurate to mark the points where the line of the curve strikes each horizontal and vertical line. The larger set of squares in Illus. 14 are four times the size of the squares in the left-hand corner of the illustration.

DRAWINGS OF TURNINGS

The drawings of an object turned on a wood lathe should not only show the shape of the object, but also give the length and diameter at critical points (Illus. 15). Often, only half of the shape is shown, since both sides are the same. Note that the length measurements are given on one side and the diameters on the other.

LAYOUT TOOLS

Using the proper tools for layout will make a job easier, more enjoyable, and probably result in a better end product. The tools discussed below are layout tools useful not only in toymaking but also in other areas of woodworking.

The French curve (Illus. 16) is used extensively in toymaking as well as in furniture layout. It can be purchased in an infinite number of shapes and sizes and is useful in drawing smooth, flowing curves of irregular shapes.

A quality bow compass is very useful in laying out small circles and arcs (Illus. 17). The less expensive compass that school children use is not recommended.

Trammel points are useful in drawing large circles or arcs (Illus. 18).

Adjustable triangles (Illus. 19) are useful for accurately laying out angles. The degree of accuracy and ease of use make these triangles much better than a protractor.

Circle templates are also very useful in the design and layout of small toy projects. They are relatively inexpensive and a quick way to draw small circles or arcs (Illus. 20).

Common woodworking layout tools used for toymaking also include the tape measure, folding ruler, try square, framing square, and marking gauge.

Illus. 15. Drawings of turning.

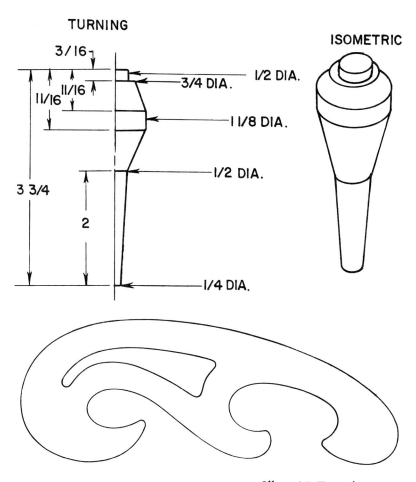

TURNING

3/16

11/16 11/16

1/2 DIA.
3/4 DIA.

1 1/8 DIA.

1/2 DIA.

3 3/4

2

1/4 DIA.

ISOMETRIC

Illus. 16. French curve.

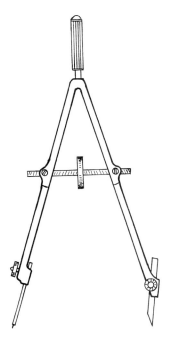

Illus. 17. Bow compass.

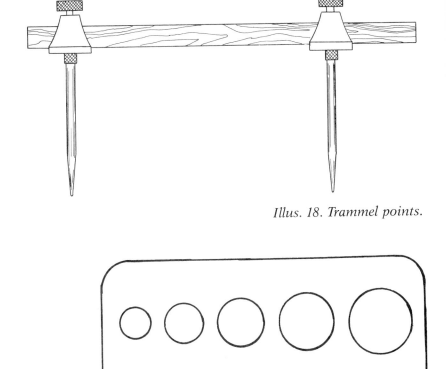

Illus. 18. Trammel points.

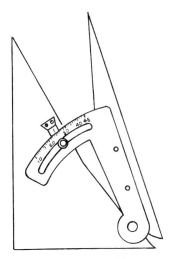

Illus. 19. Adjustable triangle.

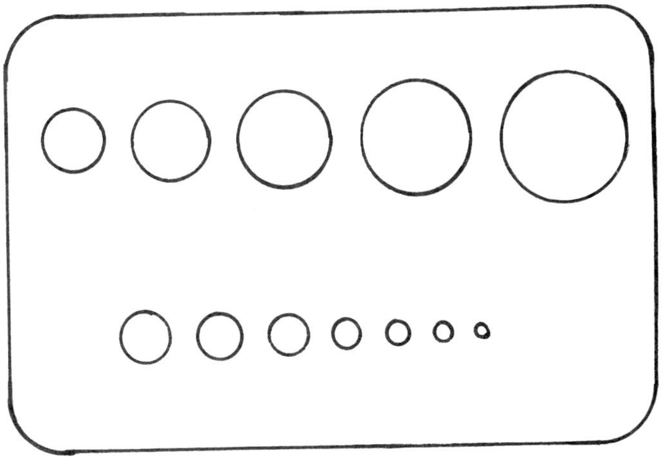

Illus. 20. Circle template.

Tools

Today, most hand-tool operations can be performed with more efficiency and with less required skill because they can be done with power machines. For example, machines are now designed to cut curves, which for years was strictly a hand-tool operation done with the compass, keyhole, and coping saws. Also, the hand plane's operations of straightening, squaring, and smoothing can now be easily performed with a jointer. Other hand-tool operations—such as grinding, shaping, mortising, and sanding—are also done with machines.

One must remember, however, that the use of power machines also has drawbacks. Though an operation may be performed quickly, mistakes can also be made quickly. Also, the risk of injury increases when power machines are used.

An additional drawback is that the more one uses power machines, the less skill he develops and the less pride he takes in a handmade project. Each individual woodworker must compromise between hand-tool and power-tool woodworking; this compromise can be determined at the point where aesthetic and economic needs are both being met.

In this chapter, I will discuss woodworking machines that are useful in toymaking, furniture making, and many other areas of woodworking. However, you may not need to use many of the machines or much of the power equipment, depending on your toymaking requirements and whether your projects are individually made or mass-produced.

SABRE SAW

The sabre saw (also called a bayonet saw or electric jigsaw) does the same operation as the hand coping saw. It can be used to cut inside or outside curves. Because the sabre saw is lightweight and most models are less expensive than the table jigsaw, it is popular among home woodworkers—especially those who carry their tools to the job, such as carpenters.

The size of the sabre saw is determined by the length of the stroke and by the motor size. Stroke lengths vary from one-half inch to one inch. The longer the stroke, the more efficient the cutting action.

The cutting speed of the sabre saw is determined by the number of strokes per minute. Sabre saws commonly operate at approximately 4,200 strokes per minute.

The handle on the sabre saw usually contains the off-on switch, and may also have a variable-speed control. The case contains the motor. The base is adjustable on most models for cutting angles. Blades are made to cut a wide range of materials, such as plastic, metals, woods, etc.

Safety Guidelines

1. Avoid loose clothing (such as neckties and the strings on sweat pants). Long hair and dangling jewelry can also be hazardous.

2. When cutting small pieces of work, clamp the work down; this prevents any chance of a hand slipping into the blade.

3. Keep both hands on the case of the saw; not only will this ensure a good grip, it

will always keep your hand away from the blade.

4. Select the correct blade for the material being cut.

5. Keep power equipment in a secure place away from inexperienced operators, and especially children.

6. Wear appropriate eye protection.

PORTABLE BELT SANDER

The portable belt sander is very useful in making wooden toys. It is often used for sanding contours and plugs, and for general sanding operations.

The portable belt sander has a handle that usually houses the off-on switch. A knob often provided in the front portion of the machine allows the operator to hold it with both hands. The back wheel or drive wheel is connected directly or by pulley to the motor. The front wheel or idler wheel may be used to adjust the belt to run true and to not come off the wheels. Most portable belt sanders are equipped with dust bags, which are a great advantage in decreasing the amount of dust created when the machine is being used.

Common sizes of portable belt sanders are 2″ × 21″, 3″ × 24″, 3″ × 27″, 4″ × 22″, and 4½″ × 26″. These sizes tell the width (small number) and the length (large number) of the sanding belt.

Safety Guidelines

1. Do not sand with the cord dangling in front of the belt sander. It can easily become entangled and cut by the belt, causing an electrical shock and damage to the cord.

2. Avoid loose clothing, long hair, loose jewelry, or other objects that can become entangled in the belt.

3. Most sanders are equipped with a switch that holds the sander in an on position. Always lay the sander on its side when you plug it in, in case this switch has inad-

vertently been left in the on position. If you do not lay the sander on its side when plugging it in, and it is left in the on position, it could jump or jerk itself off the table, causing injury to the operator and damage to the sander.

4. Belts are marked with an arrow indicating the correct direction they should be put on the sander. Using an indirect direction may cause the belt to break.

5. As with other power equipment, keep the belt sander out of the reach of children.

6. Unplug the belt sander when changing belts.

7. Wear appropriate eye protection.

ORBITAL SANDER

The orbital sander (often called a finish sander) is used to produce a scratch-free finish on wood, plastic, metals, and other materials. These sanders operate with an orbital (circular pattern) or a straight and back-and-forth motion.

Safety Guidelines

1. Unplug the sander when changing sanding sheets.

2. Wear appropriate eye protection.

PORTABLE ROUTER

The router is used for cutting a variety of curved edges. It can also be used to make V-cuts, dadoes, rabbet joints, grooves, dovetail joints, a multitude of fixtures and jigs used for special operations, and to trim Formica™.

The size of the router is determined by the size of the motor, which commonly ranges from ¼ to 2½ horsepower. Router size is also determined by the diameter of the bit shank the router is designed to use. The sizes vary from ¼ to ½ inch.

Routers run at speeds from 16,000 to 27,000. This high-speed cutting action, when used correctly, produces a very fine cut that requires little sanding.

The motor directly drives the router's bit. Most routers have two handles, one which houses the off-on switch. A depth adjustment adjusts the depth of the cut.

One book that explores all aspects of router use is *Router Handbook* by Patrick Spielman (Sterling Publishing Co., Two Park Avenue, New York, New York 10016).

Safety Guidelines

1. Always wear safety glasses or goggles. A face shield will offer added protection from chips, knots, or pieces of wood that can be thrown out of the router.

2. Always keep both hands on the router. *Never* try to hold the router in one hand and a board in the other.

3. Unplug the router when changing bits.

4. When making deep cuts, make several passes, increasing the cut's depth on each pass. Not only is this a safer method, it will also produce better-quality work.

5. Make sure the router has completely stopped before laying it down.

PORTABLE ELECTRIC HANDSAW

The portable electric handsaw performs the same basic operations as a hand ripsaw or hand crosscut saw. Because it is lightweight and can be easily carried, it is popular among carpenters and contractors. It can perform many of the same operations as the radial arm saw and the table saw. These include the following: ripping, crosscutting, and cutting grooves, dadoes, dovetails, and rabbets. A wide variety of blades are available to cut wood, slate, metal, marble, and a countless array of other materials.

The size of the portable handsaw is determined by the recommended blade diameter, which ranges from 4½ to 10 inches. Generally, the motors range in size from ⅙ to 1½ horsepower.

The off-on trigger is located in the handle. Most saws have a depth gauge that sets the depth of cut, and an angle adjustment to adjust cutting from 0 to 45°. The saw should have a safety guard that covers the blade.

Safety Guidelines

1. Whenever possible, hold both hands on the saw. Holding a small board with one hand and the saw with the other is very dangerous. The saw may kick back, jerking your hand into the blade. This can be avoided by simply clamping the board to a workbench and holding both hands on the saw.

2. Take care not to saw through the cord. This is easier to do than you might think, and can cause a serious electrical shock.

3. Always unplug the saw when changing blades or making adjustments.

4. Wear eye protection.

5. Make sure the safety guard is working properly.

6. Adjust the saw's blade so that it protrudes ⅛ to ¼ inch past the piece of wood being cut.

ELECTRIC HAND DRILL

The electric hand drill can be used to drill holes in wood, metal, plastic, concrete, and a variety of other materials. It can be used to sand, polish, buff, grind, and, used with a hole saw, to make wooden wheels for toys. Also, an endless number of accessories for it can be purchased.

The size of an electric hand drill is (like a drill press) determined by the chuck size. For example, if the chuck will hold a ½-inch bit, it's referred to as a ½-inch chuck. Common electric hand-drill sizes are ¼, ⅜, and ½ inch. The size of the motor is also an important factor when purchasing an electric hand drill. Some drills offer a reverse position as well as variable speeds.

The parts of an electric hand drill consist of a handle containing an on-off switch, and the body or case, which contain the motor and the chuck.

Safety Guidelines

1. Avoid loose clothing, jewelry, and long hair, which can become entangled in the chuck.

2. Make sure the bit is centered correctly in the chuck.

3. Wear proper eye protection. Bits sometimes break, throwing small pieces of metal that can cause serious eye damage.

BAND SAW

The band saw (Illus. 21) derives its name from its endless steel blade, which is shaped like a rubber band. The blade is one continuous strip or band of metal with teeth cut on one side. The band saw can be used to cut curves, rip stock, and resaw stock.

The size of the band saw is determined by the diameter of the wheels. A band saw with a 14-inch-diameter wheel, for example, is referred to as a 14-inch band saw. Common band saws for home use range in size from 10 to 14 inches. Schools, cabinet shops, and furniture makers often use band saws up to 20 inches. In woodworking industries, large band saws measuring 36 inches are often used, and often the machine stands several feet higher than the operator.

One of the basic parts on a band saw is the upper wheel, which the blade revolves around, and which is adjustable up and down to tighten or loosen the blade. This wheel can also be adjusted from side to side, which tilts the wheel towards the back or front and keeps the blade running correctly in the approximate center of the wheel. There is no source of power on the upper wheel.

The lower wheel is not movable vertically, and is usually connected to the motor by one or more belts. The blade rotates around these two wheels. Some models have a plastic safety guard. This guard should be kept within ¼ of an inch from the stock being cut. The table on most band saws tilts to 45° for cutting angles. Smaller band saws have sheet-metal stands or bases; larger models have massive cast-iron frameworks.

Practical blade sizes for toymaking range from widths of ⅛ to ½ inch. The smaller blades cut a sharper curve, but also tend to break more easily.

Safety Guidelines

1. The guide should be adjusted ⅛ to ¼ inch above the wood. This makes it difficult for a finger to slip in between the wood and the guide.

2. Avoid loose clothing, long hair, jewelry, and other objects that can become entangled in the blade.

3. Do not stand directly on the side of the band saw. Occasionally, when a blade breaks it may hit the table and fly out of the side of the saw, hitting the person standing on the side. Fortunately, this rarely happens because the blade usually stays inside the guards.

4. Try to keep your hands to the side of the blade, rather than directly in front of the blade.

5. Hold the stock firmly.

6. When cutting round stock, use a V-block. This helps prevent the stock from rolling and possibly jerking your hand into the blade.

7. When backing the blade out of its saw kerf, do not use force or a jerking motion; this could cause the blade to come off its wheels.

8. Make sure the tension is adjusted properly; consult your owner's manual.

9. A beginner learning to cut curves should learn on a slower-cutting table jig-

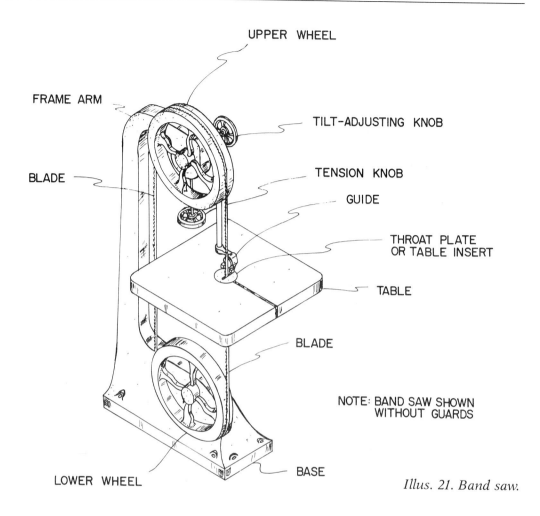

Illus. 21. Band saw.

saw. A mistake on a jigsaw is less serious than the same mistake made on a band saw. Having taught woodworking for fifteen years, I have always had students acquire skills on a jigsaw for a year or so before working with a band saw.

JOINTER

The jointer (Illus. 22) performs the same basic operation as a hand plane; that is, it cuts the edge or face of a board smooth and square in relation to an adjacent side or edge. The jointer does not perform the same operation as the planer or surfacer.

The planer will make two opposite sides of a board parallel. The jointer is not designed to do this, though some manufacturers would lead one to believe it can.

The jointer can also be used for a variety of special jobs, such as cutting rabbets, tapering, bevelling, chamfering, and making cuts in raised panelled doors.

Several essential parts make up a jointer. The front table is adjustable, and is normally adjusted to a lower level than the back table. The distance between the front table and the back table (measured vertically) determines the depth of cut. The

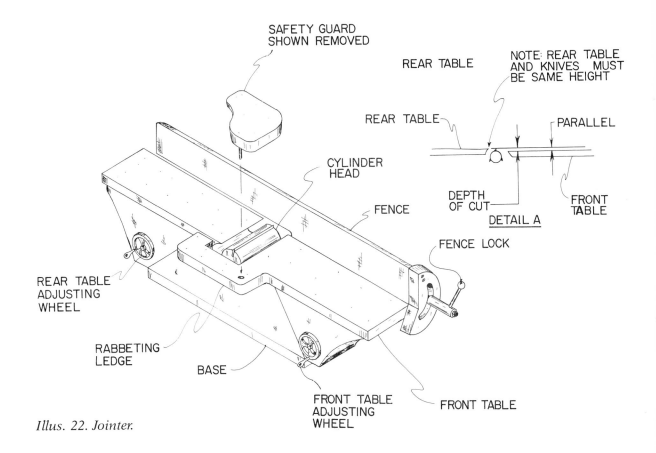

Illus. 22. Jointer.

rear table is also adjustable on many models for special operations, but normally is at the exact height as the jointer knives (blades). The knives, usually three or four, rotate on a cylinder. The length of the knives determines the size of the jointer. Thus, a jointer with 6-inch knives is referred to as a six-inch jointer; the widest board it could cut would be 6 inches wide.

Jointer sizes vary from the small 4-inch jointer, commonly used in home workshops, to the common 6- and 8-inch jointers found in many schools. Jointers found in industrial and cabinetmakers' shops are often as large as 10, 12, 14, and 16 inches.

The fence of a jointer can be adjusted for the width of a cut and can be slanted for cutting angles. The fence is also equipped with a lock to secure it in a permanent

position. The rabbeting ledge is used for cutting a rabbet joint, a joint commonly used on the edge of kitchen cabinet doors and on the backs of many projects. The safety guard swings over the blade. The motor is connected to the cylinder by means of one or two belts, and is usually located in the jointer's base.

Safety Guidelines

1. Always keep the safety guard in working order. On some jointers, the safety guard must be removed when cutting a rabbet joint.

2. Adjust the fence so that only the needed portion of the blade is exposed; that is, if one is jointing the edge of a 1-inch-wide board on a 6-inch jointer, the fence should be adjusted to cover the other

5 inches. This is a safer procedure for the beginner than leaving all 6 inches of the blade exposed.

3. When jointing the edge of narrow boards (less than 4 inches), reach across the blade. Always keep one hand on the board.

4. Only joint boards longer than 12 inches. If a shorter board is needed, joint a long board and then cut a short section off. This method may seem wasteful, but it is safer, and safety must be your first concern when performing any operation, especially when using machines.

5. Use a push shoe or block when jointing a board's face. Though a push stick is recommended for the table saw—and some manufacturers sell and advertise them for use on a jointer—do *not* use it on a jointer. There is the chance that it can jerk your hand into the blade, split the stick in two, and cause injury. Also, if the stick is being held in a near-vertical position, slips off the board, and falls into the jointer's throat (area where the knives are exposed), it can be kicked back with extreme force. If the push block slips on the board, however, it will only react as another board because of its length and because it is being held flat, and it will *not* kick back.

6. Make sure all adjustments are made and secured before the power is turned on.

7. Generally, do not cut more than ⅛ of an inch on each cut. Several small cuts are safer and will produce a smoother edge than one large deep cut. One common exception to this would be when cutting a rabbet joint. Rabbet joints for kitchen cabinets are usually cut ¼ of an inch deep by ⅜ of an inch wide to receive common kitchen cabinet hinges.

8. Hold the board firmly; always keep one hand on the board.

9. Jointers can kick a board back. Do not stand behind a jointer or let anyone stand in that position. Be especially careful when curious children are around.

10. When planing end grain, make sure the board is at least 12 inches wide. Make two cuts, both ending in the center of the board. If one cut is made, the board will probably split, causing damage to the board and possible injury to the operator.

11. Check the board for defects such as knots and, especially, nails.

12. The jointer should be kept in a place secured from children.

PLANER

The planer (also known as a thickness planer or surfacer) smooths the face of a piece of wood and cuts it to an even thickness, which means that the opposite faces are parallel (Illus. 23). The planer does not make the adjacent surfaces of a board square, as does the jointer. Planers are expensive, and not many woodworkers own one.

The planer has two table rollers which, on small models, have no power connected to them. These rollers allow the stock to slide smoothly over the lower table, which is at the same height as the rollers. On the top section of the planer there is a corrugated infeed roller that pulls the board into the planer. On better models, this corrugated roller is divided into sections; each section is allowed to press upon the board at various thicknesses. Once the infeed roller grabs the board, the board is cut smooth on its top surface by knives that rotate in the cutterhead. Next, the board is pulled again by an outfeed roller, a smooth roller that will not leave marks on the board, as often is the case with the corrugated infeed roller.

Between the cutterhead and the infeed roller is a chip breaker that holds the stock firmly against the table and prevents the

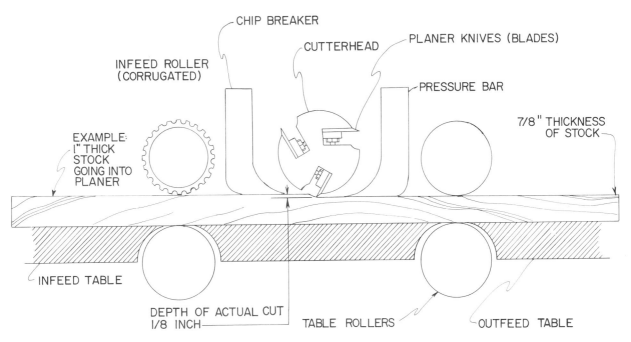

CHIP BREAKER

CUTTERHEAD

PLANER KNIVES (BLADES)

INFEED ROLLER
(CORRUGATED)

PRESSURE BAR

7/8" THICKNESS
OF STOCK

EXAMPLE:
1" THICK
STOCK
GOING INTO
PLANER

INFEED TABLE

DEPTH OF ACTUAL CUT
1/8 INCH

TABLE ROLLERS

OUTFEED TABLE

Illus. 23. Planer.

wood from being torn or chipped. The pressure bar holds the wood down on the table once it has cleared the cutterhead and chip breaker. The piece of stock to be planed should be long enough to reach from the infeed roller to the outfeed roller; this distance will vary, depending on the size of the particular planer.

The size of the planer is determined by the width of the table and by the maximum thickness the planer will accept. For example, a 13 × 6-inch planer will plane a board 13 inches wide and 6 inches thick. The length of the board being planed is limited only to the amount of room in front and behind the machine. Common sizes of planers range from the 13 × 6-inch planers commonly found in schools to larger models with a capacity to handle stock as large as 12 × 56 inches.

Safety Guidelines

1. Do not look into the planer while it is operating. Like a table saw or a jointer, the planer can kick back or throw small chips back towards the operator.

2. Keep fingers clear of the table. When the board is grabbed by the infeed rollers, the stock will be forced flat onto the table. Fingers placed under the stock can easily be smashed between the stock and the table.

3. The boards should be at least 1 inch longer than the distance between the centers of the infeed and outfeed rollers.

4. Stand to the side of the planer to avoid being hit by stock that is kicked back.

5. Check the board for loose knots, and especially for nails, staples, and other metal objects. Nails thrown from the planer can cause serious injury and chip the planer's knives.

6. The stock to be surfaced should have one true, flat side that should rest on the tables. A true, flat surface can be made on the jointer.

7. When planing long stock, have a second person help support the stock as it feeds in and out of the planer.

JIGSAW

The jigsaw (sometimes called a scroll saw) is a very safe and efficient machine for cutting inside and outside curves (Illus. 24). Jigsaws can cut a very small radius. They are excellent for teaching a beginner, young or old, to cut a curve. As a woodworking teacher, I greatly prefer that a person develop skills and safety practices on the jigsaw before learning to operate a band saw. Many of the toy parts and all of the jigsaw puzzles shown on pages 143–160 were cut on a table jigsaw.

The jigsaw's parts consist of a frame and base. The tension sleeve keeps the blade tight by means of a spring pulling upwards. The upper and lower chucks hold the blade. The table on many models tilts to 45° for cutting angles. A hold-down device that is similar to the pressure foot on a sewing machine keeps the board from bouncing up and down. The power is derived from a motor that drives the lower chuck.

The size of a jigsaw is determined by the distance from the machine's frame to the blade. Also, you should consider the thickness of the stock the machine will cut.

Safety Guidelines
1. Make sure the teeth on the jigsaw blade point down.
2. Adjust the hold-down firmly against the board, but allow for easy movement of the stock.
3. Unplug the machine when changing blades or making other adjustments.

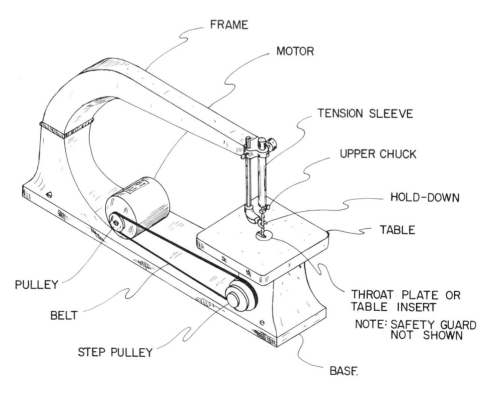

Illus. 24. Jigsaw.

4. As with most other machines, tuck in loose clothing, long hair, dangling jewelry, or anything else that might get caught in the blade.

DRILL PRESS

The drill press (Illus. 25) is not only used by the toy maker for drilling holes, but, when used with a variety of special bits and cutters, it can also perform other oper-ations. Many of the wheels in this book were made on the drill press using a hole saw. Plugs are often made with a plug cut-ter to cover screwheads. Operations that are possible include routing, shaping an edge, countersinking, sanding, mortising, cutting reeds and flutes, and, with special attachments and jigs, countless other operations.

The head section on the drill press

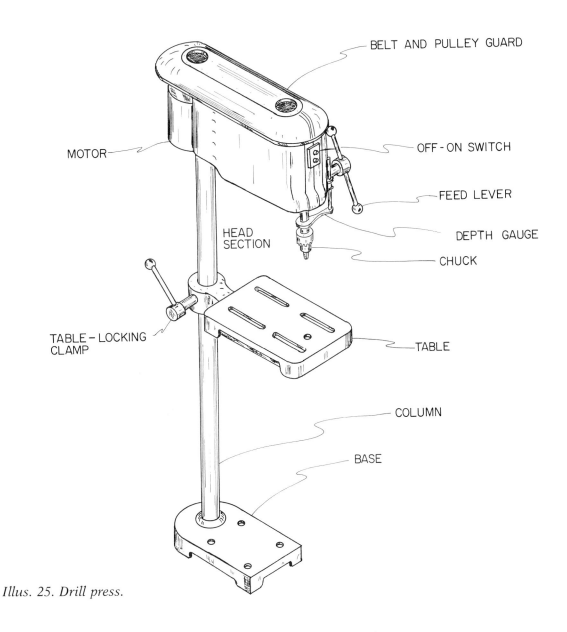

Illus. 25. Drill press.

houses the pulleys for changing the speeds. The feed lever lowers or raises the chuck and its bit. The motor is usually at the rear of the drill press, and connected to the shaft that turns the chuck by one or more pulleys. The chuck holds various bits; its size indicates the largest shaft it will hold. Common sizes of drill press chucks are ½ and ¾ inches. The column connects the drill press head to the floor or to a bench base. The table is adjustable vertically on the column; most tables can rotate 360°.

The size of the drill press is determined by the distance from the front of the column to the center of the chuck. Common sizes vary from 12 to 20 inches. The speeds at which drill presses run vary from about 300 to 6,000 rpm. When buying a drill press, also consider the chuck size. For the toy maker or furniture maker, a drill press with a half-inch chuck is recommended.

Safety Guidelines

1. Loose clothing, jewelry, long hair, and other loose articles can easily get caught in a turning chuck or bit. Tuck these articles in to avoid a dangerous situation.

2. Always wear eye protection, such as safety glasses or a face shield.

3. Don't touch the chuck until the machine has come to a complete stop. Rings can get caught in the chuck's teeth or in a burr of metal. The ring could be jerked, which could lead to a serious injury.

4. Be sure to remove the chuck key from the chuck. Some of the newer chuck keys remove themselves with a spring mechanism, which is an added safety feature. A chuck key left in a chuck can be thrown with a great deal of force when the drill press is turned on, causing serious injury to the operator or others.

5. Use the manufacturer's recommended speed for the various types of drill bits.

6. Since small pieces can be jerked out of the operator's hand, use clamps or home-made jigs to hold them.

7. When drilling deep holes, back the bit out, occasionally clearing the hole of wood shavings that would otherwise build up and make it difficult to remove the bit.

8. Keep the drill press in a location secured from children.

TABLE SAW

The table saw (Illus. 26) offers a wide range of operations suited to the toy maker, furniture maker, or cabinetmaker. The size of the table saw is determined by the largest blade recommended to be used on the particular saw. Thus, the 8-inch table saw uses an 8-inch-diameter blade. Table saws range in size from 8 to 16 inches. The most common-size table saw used for toymaking, cabinetmaking, and furniture making is the 10-inch table saw. Schools often use a 10- or 12-inch table saw. Fourteen- and 16-inch saws are commonly found in lumber companies and light woodworking industries.

The table on the better table saw models is made of cast iron and is machined to a true, flat surface. Other, less expensive models may have cast-aluminum or sheet-metal tables. Different throat plates are available for various blade widths, such as, for example, the different widths of a dado blade. The blade may be attached directly to the motor or, on better saws, driven by one or more belts connecting a motor to the saw's arbor. The saw arbor is the shaft that the blade is attached to. Common sizes of arbors are ½-, ⅝-, and ¾-inch diameters. The base of the table saw can be designed to sit on the floor or, on smaller models, to be placed on a bench.

The blade on most table saws can be tilted with a tilting hand wheel. Most blades tilt from a perpendicular position to 45° in relation to the table's top. On some

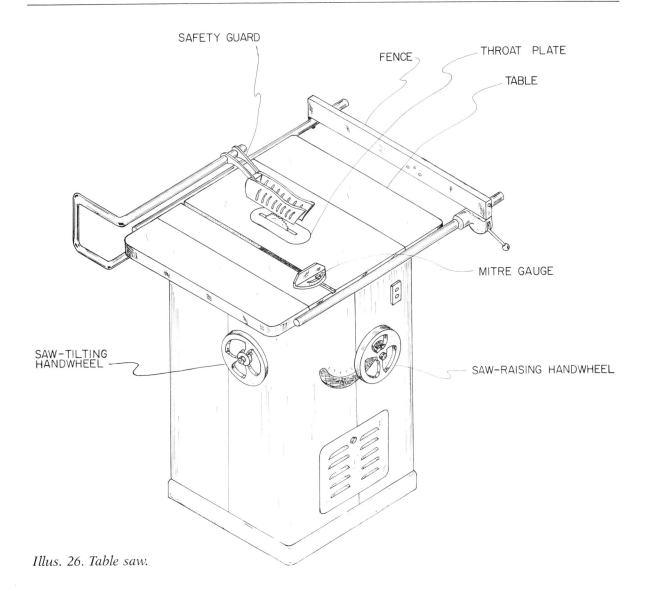

SAFETY GUARD

FENCE

THROAT PLATE

TABLE

MITRE GAUGE

SAW-TILTING HANDWHEEL

SAW-RAISING HANDWHEEL

Illus. 26. Table saw.

models, the blade stays stationary and the table tilts. The blade can also be raised and lowered to adjust the depth of the cut.

The fence is used mainly for ripping operations, and should be parallel to the blade. The mitre gauge slides in a groove on the table's top, and is used for crosscutting; it can be adjusted for cutting various angles.

Table saws are sold with a variety of different types of safety guards. The use of a safety guard is highly recommended.

Become thoroughly acquainted with your table saw; make sure you understand all of its parts. Read and study in depth books on woodworking and consult an experienced, reputable woodworker for some hands-on advice. One book that explores all aspects of table saw use is *Table Saw Techniques* by Roger Cliffe (Sterling Publishing Co., Two Park Avenue, New York, New York 10016).

A variety of blades are available for use on the table saw. The moulding head cutter is used to cut various shapes of moulding. The dado blade is used to cut a wide saw kerf usually up to a width of ¾ to 1 inch. The crosscut blade is used for cutting across or perpendicular to the direction of the grain. The ripsaw blade is used to cut with the grain. A combination blade is designed to be used for ripping or cross-cutting operations. The plywood blade is made exclusively for cutting plywood. It will produce a very fine, smooth cut with little or no splitting of the veneered layers. Some blades have carbide teeth that cut smoothly and efficiently; these blades stay sharp several times longer than the conventional steel blade.

Safety Guidelines

1. Keep the floor clean. Sawdust is slippery and can cause you to slip and fall.

2. Lower the blade when you are finished with the saw. An exposed blade protruding out of the saw's throat plate can be hazardous if fallen on. The saw does not have to be running to cause an injury.

3. Use a safety guard.

4. The blade should be adjusted so that it is ⅛ to ¼ inch above the wood being cut. Letting the blade protrude several inches above the wood exposes a potentially dangerous blade needlessly, a situation that could cause a very serious injury.

5. Make any adjustments, such as lowering, raising, or tilting the blade, only when the saw is not running.

6. When changing the blade, unplug the saw. Lay the plug on top of the table within your sight; this visually assures you that the saw cannot be started.

7. Don't stand directly behind the saw. Stand slightly to one side of the blade. Also, do not let anyone else stand behind the table saw. A piece of stock can become wedged between the saw's blade and the

fence and be kicked back with extreme force, causing serious injury to anyone directly behind the table saw.

8. Do not reach over the saw's blade to hold the board after it has been cut. If the board kicks back, your hand or finger can be pulled back into the blade.

9. Never cut "freehand." Cutting wood on a table saw without the use of any of the devices available that ensure straight cuts can lead to a serious accident. The table saw is equipped with a rip fence and mitre gauge, which are designed to hold the board in a straight line while it is being cut. They should be used.

10. Tuck in loose clothing, jewelry, long hair, and other articles that may get caught in a spinning blade. Do not wear a tie around machinery with moving parts, such as the table saw.

11. Don't leave the table saw until the blade has completely stopped turning. This is particularly important when working with other people, especially the inexperienced.

12. Keep the blade sharp and the teeth set properly. Dull blades tend to bind, cut slowly, and burn, which are all factors that can result in kick-back situations.

13. Make sure the fence and the mitre gauge are adjusted properly. The fence should be tightened so that it does not move during an operation. The mitre gauge should slide smoothly at right angles to the blade.

14. Hold the stock firmly against the fence or mitre gauge.

15. Use a push stick when ripping narrow stock—stock less than 4 inches wide.

16. The stock being cut on the table saw should be at least the length of the table saw's diameter. For example, do not rip a board shorter than 10 inches on a 10-inch table saw. Though this can be done, a short board can easily twist and be kicked back.

17. Give the saw time to reach its full speed before beginning a cut.

18. Don't be distracted by others when using a table saw. Always give the table saw your full attention to ensure the safest possible operation.

19. Keep your table saw in an area unaccessible to small children or other untrained persons.

WOOD LATHE

The wood lathe (Illus. 27) is designed to make round objects in wood and many other materials. It, more than any other woodworking machine, gives the operator much more leeway for safe experimentation and for creating new shapes and designs.

The wood lathe is the oldest power woodworking machine. It has been powered by water, foot power from a treadle mechanism, and even by hand by an apprentice. In today's modern industry, the automatic or production lathe produces turnings many times faster than those turned by hand. This type of situation in industry leaves little room for an operator to take pride in his work or to be creative. The wood lathe when used by an individual is mainly used by patternmakers, furniture makers, cabinetmakers, toy makers, antique restorers, and those woodworkers interested in making one piece at a time.

The lathe consists of several basic parts. The headstock houses the motor or a shaft with a pulley connected to the motor. The

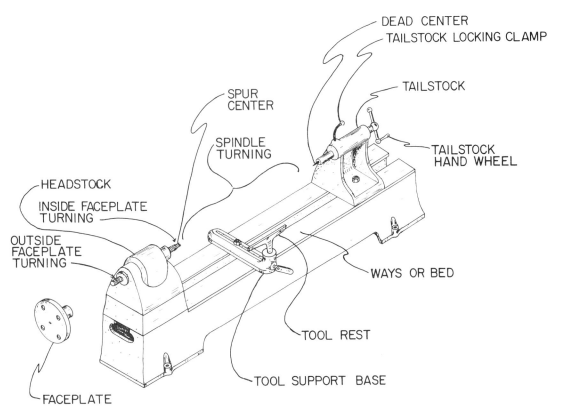

Illus. 27. Wood lathe.

5. Make sure the safey guard is in proper working order.

6. Secure the locking devices before turning the saw on.

7. When the saw is turned off, stand beside it until it comes to a complete stop.

8. Radial arm saws, like table saws, can throw a board, knot, or a defect if not used properly. Keep other people, especially children, safely away from the saw.

9. Wear safety glasses or other appropriate eye protection.

10. Tuck in long hair, loose clothing, and jewelry.

11. Make sure the piece of wood being cut does not contain nails, staples, or other objects that may be thrown and cause an injury.

MORTISING MACHINE

The mortising machine is used to make the mortise-and-tenon joint commonly used in fine furniture construction. It cuts a square or rectangular hole that can vary in size from ¼ to 1 inch; this hole is referred to as the mortise part of the joint. The mortising machine does not cut the tenon, which can easily be cut with the table saw or radial arm saw. The rumble seat on the Model T coupé (page 66) is a toy part that can be ideally cut with a mortising machine.

Two types of mortising machines are commonly found in industry today. The chisel mortising machine uses a drill bit inside a square chisel. The drill bit drills the hole round, while the square corners of the chisel cut the hole square. The chain mortising machine works in the same fashion as a chain saw; it is mounted vertically and pushed vertically into a piece of wood. The result is a square hole with a round bottom. This type of machine is of little use to the individual toy maker, but is very efficient in an industrial setting.

A chisel mortising attachment that does a good job for the home craftsman can be bought for most drill presses. However, remember that mortising (cutting square holes) can also be done easily by hand with a drill press, a good sharp chisel, a mallet, and a little skill that develops through practice. A chisel mortising attachment, although handy to have, is not necessary to produce toys or beautiful furniture.

Safety Guidelines

1. Tuck in long hair, loose clothing, jewelry, and other articles that can become entangled in the chisel and bit.

2. Wear appropriate eye protection.

3. Use a hold-down device or clamp the stock to the table instead of trying to hold it with your hand.

4. Make sure you are using the correct-size bit for the chisel being used. The bit should extend below the chisel approximately ¹⁄₁₆ of an inch.

5. When the machine is turned off, stand beside it until the bit has completely stopped turning.

SPINDLE SANDER

The spindle sander (also called the vertical drum sander) is designed to sand irregular curves. On better machines, the spindle has an oscillating (up and down) motion that helps eliminate sanding lines that are made if the drum does not oscillate.

Spindle sanders range in size from ½ to 6 inches in diameter. The parts of a spindle sander are the base, the table (which tilts on better models), the drum (which oscillates on better models), and the spindle nut, which holds the sandpaper firmly on the spindle.

Safety Guidelines

1. Make sure the spindle nut is tightened securely.

2. Keep fingers clear of the throat. Avoid sanding very small pieces that could fall in between the throat and the spindle; they could cause your fingers to jerk, and possibly an accident.

3. Avoid loose clothing, jewelry, and long hair.

4. Wear eye protection.

5. Make holding jigs to hold small parts.

STATIONARY DISC SANDER

The stationary disc sander (Illus. 29) can be used for smoothing and shaping wood, and is very useful for making many of the toy parts in this book. The disc sander can be either an individual machine or, as is most often the case, a combination machine with a belt sander. Special discs are available for the radial arm or table saw; with them, the operator can convert the saw to a disc sander. The abrasive disc can be bought in many grades that range from very fine to coarse. Discs are made of paper or cloth, and many have their own adhesive backing. The rotating sanding action of a disc sander leaves a circular pattern of scratches in the wood, but the finer

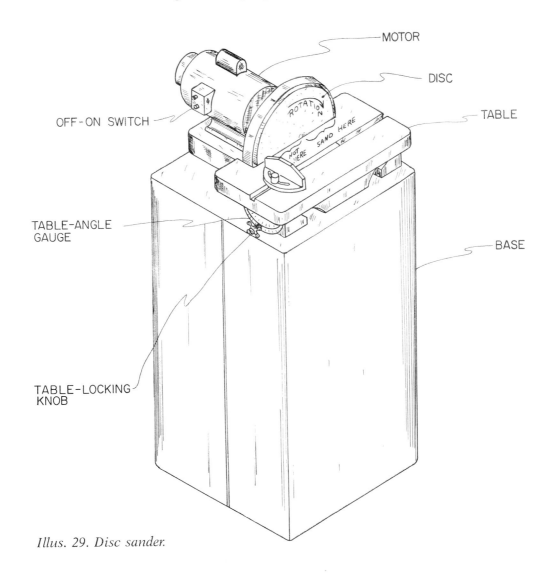

Illus. 29. Disc sander.

the scratch the easier it is to sand out by hand.

The motor is usually connected to the disc directly or, on some models, by one or more belts. An abrasive disc is attached to a metal disc. The table tilts for sanding angles. Some models include a mitre gauge similar to that used on the table saw; the mitre gauge is used for sanding angles. The base or stand on smaller models is made of sheet metal; on the larger models, it is often made of cast iron.

The size of the disc sander is determined by the diameter of the disc. Common sizes for home use are 8, 10, and 12 inches. Larger models found in schools or industries may range up to 30 inches in diameter.

Safety Guidelines

1. Sand on the side of the disc that rotates downwards, thus forcing the stock down against the table. Sanding on the side that rotates upwards could cause the stock to be thrown upwards, which could possibly jerk the operator's hand into the disc or throw the stock.

2. Sand lightly; a sanding disc in good condition requires little pressure. If the operator pushes hard against the disc, he may slip and press his hand into the disc, causing injury.

3. Make sure the abrasive disc is attached securely and is centered as closely as possible.

4. Never get a finger or hand caught between the disc and the table. A larger disc sander could pull a finger and literally sand it off.

5. Always unplug the machine when making adjustments and changing abrasive discs.

6. Avoid loose clothing, jewelry, and long hair, which can become entangled in the sanding discs.

Techniques and Tips

Although these woodworking techniques and tips will be especially useful for the novice woodworker, they will help facilitate the toymaking process for everyone.

V-BLOCK

V-blocks (Illus. 30) have been used for years as a means of holding round stock being drilled in wood, metal, or other material. The V-block can even be used to hold material that is being sawed on a band saw or, in certain cases, on a table saw.

On the drill press, the V-block ensures that the hole will line up with the center of the stock and not be off to one side, as shown in Illus. 30. Before drilling, align the drill bit with the center of the V-block. The V-block should be clamped to the table of

the drill press to maintain this position. Then round stock of almost any size can be drilled on center, as, for example, when drilling holes in the steam engine boiler for the train on page 98.

PREVENTING CHIPPING WITH A FORSTNER BIT

The Forstner bit is used extensively in the toymaking discussed throughout this book. When drilling with a Forstner bit (Illus. 31), a flat-bottomed bit, you have to take certain precautions. Shavings left under the board will cause the Forstner bit to rest unevenly and cause splitting, so they should be disposed of. Also, the stock must rest flat on a scrap piece of wood and be held firmly; this should prevent chipping

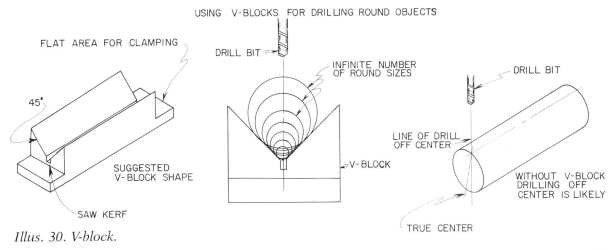

Illus. 30. V-block.

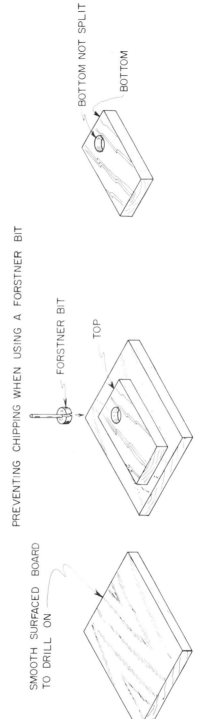

NOTICE SPLITTING

BOTTOM

BOTTOM NOT SPLIT

BOTTOM

BOTTOM, SPLIT OUT

CHIPS AND SHAVINGS UNDER BOARD MAY CAUSE THE BOTTOM TO SPLIT OUT.

TOP, SMOOTH CUT

PREVENTING CHIPPING WHEN USING A FORSTNER BIT

FORSTNER BIT

TOP

MANY PREVIOUS HOLES HAVE BEEN DRILLED HERE. THIS MAY CAUSE BOTTOM TO SPLIT OUT IF BOARD IS PLACED OVER DRILLED AREA.

SMOOTH SURFACED BOARD TO DRILL ON

Illus. 31. How to prevent chipping when using a Forstner bit.

from the bottom. Finally, it is essential to have a sharp bit. Forstner bits generally require a slower speed than other bits, and tend to burn at higher speeds, which dulls them.

INSIDE OBLONG CUTS

When making parts such as the boom for the crane on page 91, a good way to make inside cuts is to first lay out the part to be cut (Illus. 32, step one). Note that the round section of the cut is best executed not by using a jigsaw or coping saw but by drilling this portion out. A Forstner bit will produce a smooth-sided hole that will require little sanding.

Drill the holes required as shown in step two in Illus. 32. Then cut out the remaining straight sections with a coping saw or jigsaw (step three). This method should produce an oblong cut with near-perfect rounded ends (step four).

MAKING ROUND PLUGS

On the crane (page 91), thin, round pieces of walnut are used to make fake rollers. The method I use to get these pieces is very safe and efficient. First, obtain a plug cutter for the required size. Drill into the stock as shown in Illus. 33, step one. The depth to be drilled should be determined by the thickness of the plug needed. In step two, cut a thin strip to the thickness of the re-

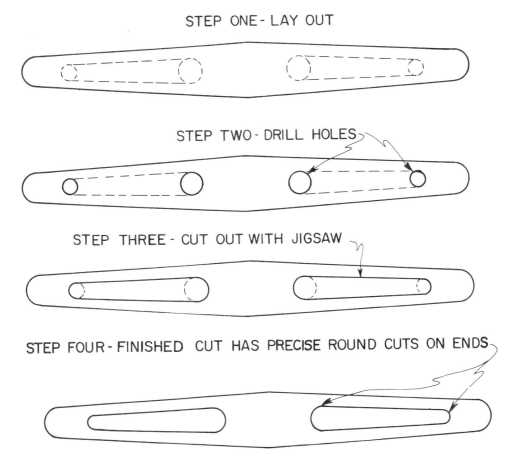

STEP ONE - LAY OUT

STEP TWO - DRILL HOLES

STEP THREE - CUT OUT WITH JIGSAW

STEP FOUR - FINISHED CUT HAS PRECISE ROUND CUTS ON ENDS

Illus. 32. Inside oblong cuts.

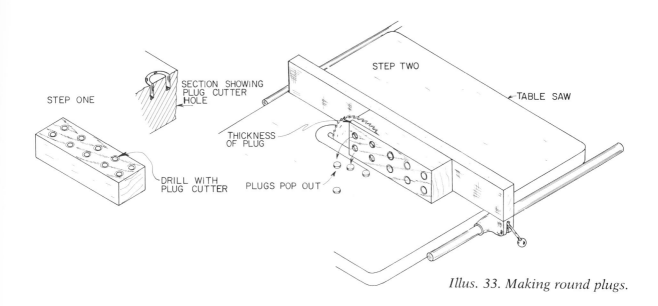

STEP ONE

SECTION SHOWING
PLUG CUTTER
HOLE

STEP TWO

TABLE SAW

THICKNESS
OF PLUG

DRILL WITH
PLUG CUTTER

PLUGS POP OUT

Illus. 33. Making round plugs.

quired plugs with the table saw. (This thin strip can also be cut on a band saw with a rip fence.) Be sure to use a push stick if you are cutting a narrow piece of wood. As the cut is made, the thin, round pieces will fall out, as shown in Illus. 33, step two.

CUTTING RABBET JOINTS

The rabbet joint is commonly found on kitchen cabinet doors and drawer fronts. It is sometimes used on fine furniture, but many times the flush-fitting door, requiring more skill, is used by the furniture maker. The small kitchen appliances discussed on pages 119–140 have rabbet edges.

The rabbet joint can be easily and safely cut on a table saw, as shown in Illus. 34. In step one, a saw kerf is cut to the desired depth. Then, in step two, a second kerf is made, resulting in a rabbet joint.

At the end of the second cut, a small piece of wood will remain uncut; it usually wedges itself between the blade and fence, causing it to kick back. This kickback is to be expected, and will not be dangerous as

long as you follow the safety rules for the table saw, and do *not* stand directly behind it. When the small piece is kicked back, it will simply fall to the floor, avoiding you completely.

You can also use a jointer to cut a rabbet joint (Illus. 35). First set the fence to the width of the cut desired. For most kitchen cabinet hinges, the standard width is ⅜ of an inch. Next, set the depth; standard hinges usually require ¼ inch. Depending on the kind of wood being used, this joint will require one or, in some cases, two cuts. Making two cuts will ensure smoother results.

The safety guard on most jointers rests on the rabbet ledge, and for this operation it must be removed. Cutting rabbet joints on end grain is not recommended for the inexperienced woodworker because the jointer will split and tear solid wood easily. Laminated plywood is better, and there will be fewer problems; however, it will also split and tear if the top layer of the veneer is in the end-grain position.

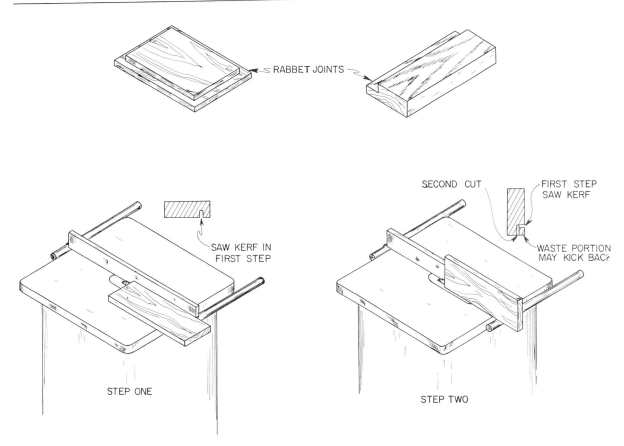

RABBET JOINTS

SAW KERF IN
FIRST STEP

STEP ONE

SECOND CUT

FIRST STEP
SAW KERF

WASTE PORTION
MAY KICK BACK

STEP TWO

Illus. 34. Cutting a rabbet joint on a table saw.

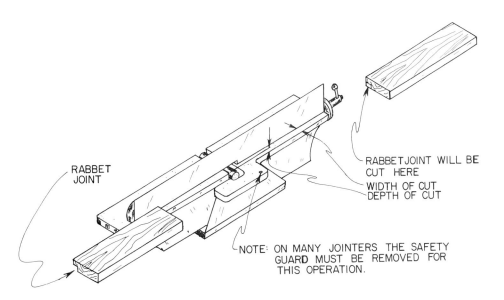

RABBET
JOINT

RABBET JOINT WILL BE
CUT HERE
WIDTH OF CUT
DEPTH OF CUT

NOTE: ON MANY JOINTERS THE SAFETY
GUARD MUST BE REMOVED FOR
THIS OPERATION.

Illus. 35. Cutting a rabbet joint with a jointer.

ADJUSTABLE SHELVES

The method of making adjustable shelves shown in Illus. 36 is occasionally found in antique furniture. It can be easily accomplished in three steps. First, lay out the overall dimensions required for the particular appliance being made. Then lay out the center line for the holes. In step two, drill the required number of holes with a drill press. Drill the holes for both boards at the same time. In step three, rip both boards down the center on the table saw, using the table saw's fence. This will leave two parts with the holes or round sections lined up exactly. The final step in Illus. 36 shows how the shelves rest on an adjustable shelf support that can easily be moved up and down.

CUTTING MORTISES

Cutting a mortise (Illus. 37) is required for the construction of the train (page 98). The process described here can also be used in fine furniture construction, where the mortise-and-tenon joint is an essential joint. This operation can be performed with either a mortising machine or a drill press with a mortise attachment.

Carving the actual shape of the hole is easy to do and can be perfected with practice. First, lay out the size of the mortise (step 1, Illus. 37). A try square and marking gauge are useful. Then, drill the holes to the required depth. (Step 2 in Illus. 37 shows the holes after they have been drilled.) A drill press is ideal for this operation since the drill bit is aligned vertically. A Forstner bit will produce a smooth-sided hole. If a drill press is not available, use a dowelling jig; it will also hold the bit square. Either an auger bit or a twist bit can be used with a dowelling jig.

Once the holes are drilled, slightly overlapping each other, use a sharp wood chisel and mallet (step 3) and carve out the overall shape of the hole. If you've never cut a mortise by hand, practise on a scrap board, preferably using the same type of wood as that being used on the project. Cutting a mortise by hand should only take minutes after you have developed some skill.

MAKING APPLIANCE KNOBS

The knob for the stove (page 119) can easily be made in four steps. Step 1 in Illus.

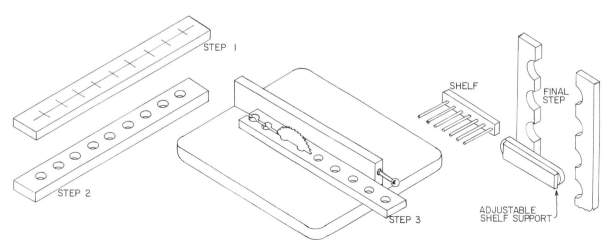

Illus. 36. Making adjustable shelves.

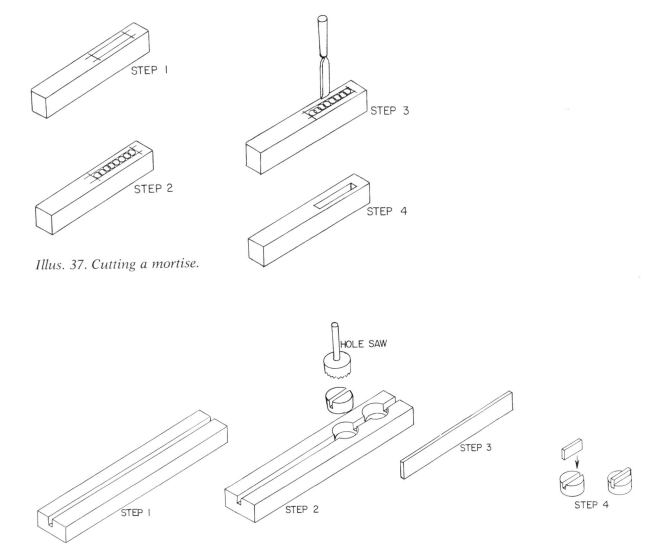

Illus. 37. Cutting a mortise.

Illus. 38. Making appliance knobs.

38 shows the board after it has been cut on the table saw; the board is long enough to make the number of knobs required. The board should also be wide enough for the knobs, and its thickness should be equal to the thickness of the knobs. Cut a groove on the table saw to the depth required and to the width of the strip shown in step 3.

In step 2, use a hole saw to cut out the round knobs; make sure the hole saw bit is placed in the center of the groove. In step 3, cut the strips that fit in the groove to their required size. To finish the knob, cut the strip to its required length and glue the strip into the knob, as shown in step 4.

MAKING THE AIRPLANE'S FUSELAGE

The fuselages for the biplane (page 169) and Piper Cub (page 176) can be made in a similar fashion (Illus. 39). In step one, lay out the shape by drawing a grid on the

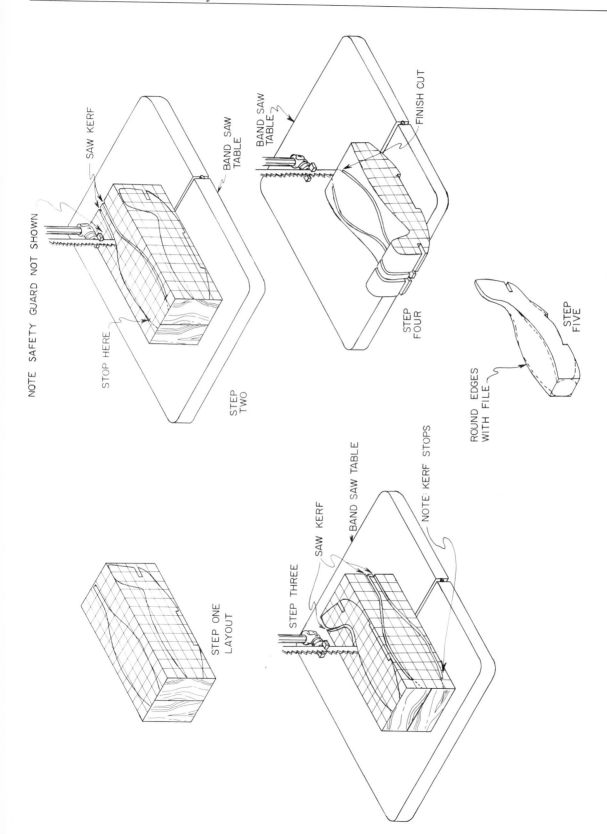

Illus. 39. Making the airplanes' fuselages.

NOTE SAFETY GUARD NOT SHOWN

SAW KERF

STOP HERE

BAND SAW TABLE

STEP TWO

BAND SAW TABLE

FINISH CUT

STEP FOUR

ROUND EDGES WITH FILE

STEP FIVE

STEP ONE LAYOUT

STEP THREE

SAW KERF

BAND SAW TABLE

NOTE: KERF STOPS

stock. Do this for the top view of the fuselage and the view of the fuselage when seen from the side. In step two, use a band saw to first cut out the shape of the top view; you should stop about a ½ inch before the end of the cut on both saw kerfs.

In step three, turn the fuselage over and complete cutting the shape out. Set the plane upright, as shown in step four, and finish the band saw cuts. This should leave the fuselage completely cut out. The corners should be rounded with a wood file to approximately a ½-inch radius (step five). This operation is basically the same as cutting the compound cuts required on a cabriole leg, a type of leg used on Early American lowboys and highboys.

MAKING SPOKE WHEELS

Spoke wheels are used on the truck and Model T sedan and coupé (pages 54, 48, and 66). Five steps are used to make these wheels (Illus. 40). In step 1, cut out the wheel with a hole saw and drill press; then lay out the position of the spokes. In step 2, drill out the recessed portion of the wheel with a Forstner bit and a drill press. Glue the axle into the wheel.

In step 3, make the hub by filing or sanding the end of a dowel rod round. Then drill

the required hole in the hub to a size that matches the dowel rod for the axle. Glue the hub over the axle so that the flat end of the hub rests upon the recessed portion of the wheel.

In step 4, drill a small hole slightly smaller than the wire brad through the wheel and into the hub. Drill as many holes as required. In step 5, drive a wire brad very gently through the wheel and into the hub. Countersink the wire brads slightly with a nail set and fill with wood filler. The axle must be inside the toy before the second wheel is put on the axle.

HOLE SAW SIZES AND WHEEL SIZES

When making wheels for wooden toys, you will use the hole saw extensively. Some hole saws have a round shaft that is actually part of the drill bit. On better models, the shaft is hex-shaped and cannot slip in the chuck.

Hole saws of different brands may produce slightly different-sized wheels due to the thickness of the hole saw's metal and the set in the saw's teeth. The chart on page 46 shows the hole saw's sizes and the approximate-size wheels it will make. All sizes are in inches.

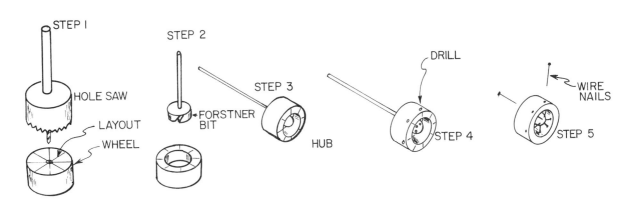

Illus. 40. Making spoke wheels.

HOLE SAW SIZE	WHEEL SIZE
3"	2¾ to 2¹³/₁₆"
2½"	2½ to 2⁵/₁₆"
2¼"	2 to 2¹/₁₆"
2 "	1¾ to 1¹³/₁₆"
1¾"	1½ to 1⁹/₁₆"
1½"	1¼ to 1⁵/₁₆"
1⅜"	1⅛ to 1³/₁₆"
1¼"	1 to 1¹/₁₆"
1"	¾ to ¹³/₁₆"
⅞"	⅝ to ¹¹/₁₆"
¾"	½ to ⁹/₁₆"

CUTTING PLYWOOD

When cutting plywood—which you will be doing when you make toy appliances—you'll notice that the veneered surface has a tendency to split and chip easily. Several techniques may help solve this problem.

One technique for cutting dadoes in plywood is to estimate the size of the saw kerf and use a knife to score the edge. In other words, make a cut along the veneer where the edge of the dado will be; this will help prevent splitting.

Another technique is to lay out the dado cuts with a pencil and then use masking tape over the cut. The masking tape should help prevent splitting. When removing the masking tape, make sure it does not lift splinters from the wood.

When using the radial arm saw, make sure you have a flat, smooth board below the board you are cutting; this will also help prevent splitting. Also, special hollow-ground plywood blades with many teeth will cut plywood smoothly.

PROJECTS

Model T Sedan

Illus. 41. See page E of the color section for a look at the Model T sedan in full color.

Key to Assembly Shown in Illus. 43

LETTER	NUMBER REQUIRED	PART	SIZE
A	1	Body	$8^{5}/_{8} \times 4^{1}/_{4} \times 3''$
B	2	Front fender	$3^{1}/_{2} \times 2^{1}/_{2} \times {}^{3}/_{4}''$
C	2	Running board	${}^{3}/_{4} \times {}^{1}/_{4} \times 2^{3}/_{4}''$
D	2	Back fender	$3^{1}/_{2} \times 3 \times {}^{3}/_{4}''$
E	1	Front bumper	${}^{7}/_{8} \times {}^{1}/_{2} \times 4''$
F	1	Back bumper	$1 \times {}^{1}/_{2} \times 4''$
G	4	Wheel	$2^{1}/_{2} \times 2^{1}/_{2} \times {}^{3}/_{4}''$
H	4	Hub	${}^{1}/_{2}''$ dowel, ${}^{1}/_{2}''$ long
I	1	Spare wheel	$2^{1}/_{2} \times 2^{1}/_{2} \times {}^{1}/_{2}''$
J	1	Spare wheel hub	${}^{1}/_{2}''$ dowel, ${}^{3}/_{8}''$ long
K	2	Headlight	${}^{1}/_{2}''$ dowel, ${}^{3}/_{8}''$ long
L	1	Back axle	${}^{1}/_{4}''$ dowel, $3^{3}/_{4}''$ long
M	1	Front axle	${}^{1}/_{4}''$ dowel, $3^{3}/_{8}''$ long
N	1	Spare tire rod	${}^{1}/_{4}''$ dowel, $1''$ long
O	1	Trunk	$1^{1}/_{8} \times 1^{3}/_{4} \times 2^{1}/_{4}''$
P	1	Radiator cap	${}^{1}/_{8}''$ dowel, $5^{5}/_{8}''$ long

TOOLS AND SUPPLIES

Drill press
Table saw
Hammer
Band saw
Straight-cutting
  router bits
Wood filler
1¼″ × No. 10
  combination drill
1¼″ × No. 10 flathead
  screws
Plug cutter
No. 2 finishing nails

Wood filler
Glue
Belt sander
Jointer
Try square
Nail set
Router
Drill bits
Hole saw
Electric hand drill

CONSTRUCTION NOTES

Part A (Illus. 42)

Lay out the view of the sedan as seen from the side. Use the router to rout out the window section. Use a twist bit and drill press to drill out the holes for parts L and M (axles). (See Illus. 44 for parts L and M.) Use the band saw to cut out the shape as seen from the side. Once this is done, drill the hole for part P (radiator cap). (See Illus. 47 for part P.) Lay out the shape of the car as seen from the top and use the band saw to cut this out. Round the edges, as shown in Illus. 43, with a wood file, then sand.

NOTE: EACH SQUARE EQUALS 1/2 INCH

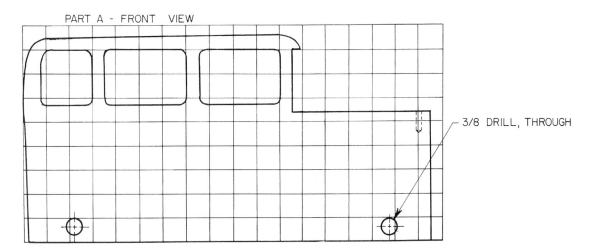

PART A - FRONT VIEW

3/8 DRILL, THROUGH

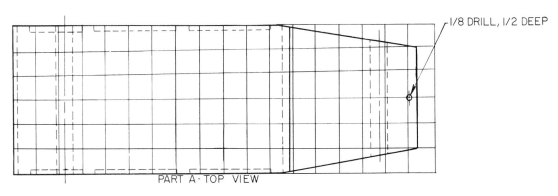

1/8 DRILL, 1/2 DEEP

PART A - TOP VIEW

Illus. 42. Part A.

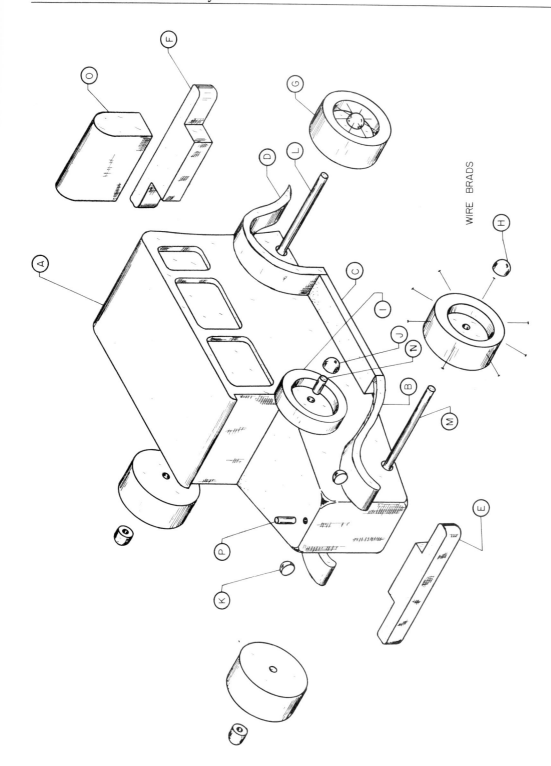

Illus. 43. Assembly for Model T sedan.

Parts G, H, I, J, L, M, N (Illus. 44)

Cut parts L, M, and N (back axle, front axle, and spare tire rod) to length from a dowel rod. The steps in making parts G, H, I, and J (wire wheel parts) are outlined in detail on page 45. Once these parts are made, glue the wheels to parts L and M (axles). Put the axles through part A and glue the wheel on the other side. Glue part N into part A, then glue part I (spare wheel) to part N.

Parts E, F, and O (Illus. 45)

Plane a board long enough for parts E and F (front and back bumpers); make sure the board is long enough to be safely used. Use a band saw to cut parts E and F out. Use an electric hand drill, and predrill holes for two No. 6 finishing nails. Glue parts E and F onto part A so that their bottoms are flush; use two finishing nails to ensure that they hold firmly. Countersink the nails with a nail set and fill with wood filler. Part O (trunk) can be cut on a band saw and should be glued to the back of part A, resting on the bumper. Use two ¼″ × No. 10 flathead wood screws to secure Part O to part A. Cover the screws with plugs and sand.

Parts B, C, and D (Illus. 46)

Parts B and D (front and back fenders) should be made from birch plywood, which will keep the pieces from breaking. Part C (running board) can be cut on the table saw. Work with a board that is longer than necessary to ensure a safer operation.

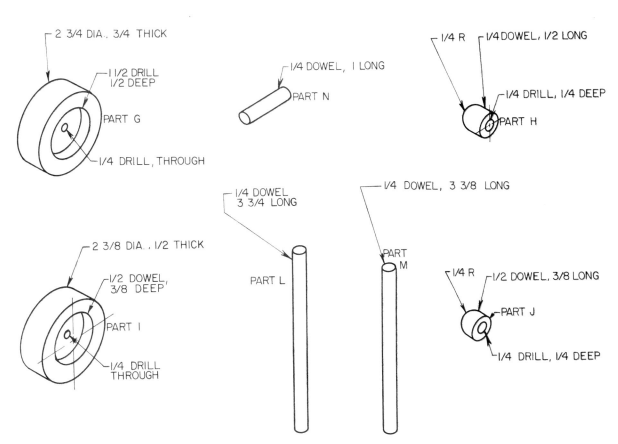

Illus. 44. Parts G, H, I, J, L, M, and N.

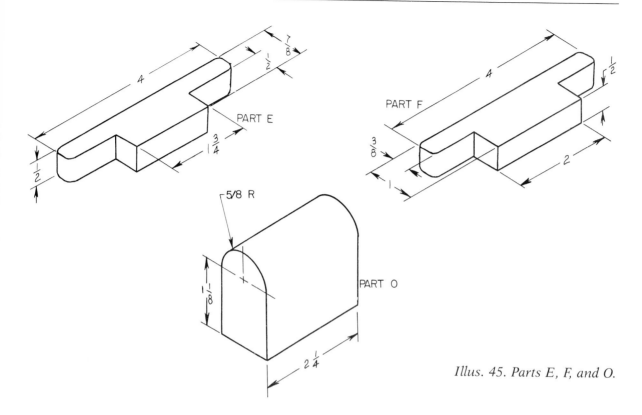

PART E

PART F

5/8 R

PART O

Illus. 45. Parts E, F, and O.

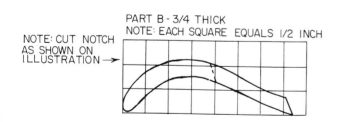

NOTE: CUT NOTCH
AS SHOWN ON
ILLUSTRATION →

PART B - 3/4 THICK
NOTE: EACH SQUARE EQUALS 1/2 INCH

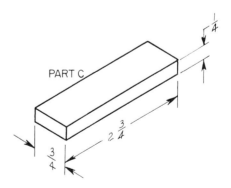

PART C

PART D - 3/4 THICK
NOTE: EACH SQUARE EQUALS 1/2 INCH

Illus. 46. Parts B, C, and D.

Once it has been cut, glue part C to part A (body) so that parts C and A are flush on the bottom. Glue parts B (front fender) and D (back fender) to part A so that they are approximately ⅛ inch above the wheel.

Parts K and P (Illus. 47)

Cut part P (radiator cap) from a dowel rod and glue it into part A so that it pro-trudes out of part A by approximately ⅛ inch. Using a dowel rod for the headlights that's long enough for a safe operation, sand the ends round with a belt or disc sander. Finish rounding by hand.

Once the headlights are made, cut them to the correct length and attach them to part A, using a No. 4 finishing nail. Be sure to predrill the hole, countersink the nail, and fill with wood filler.

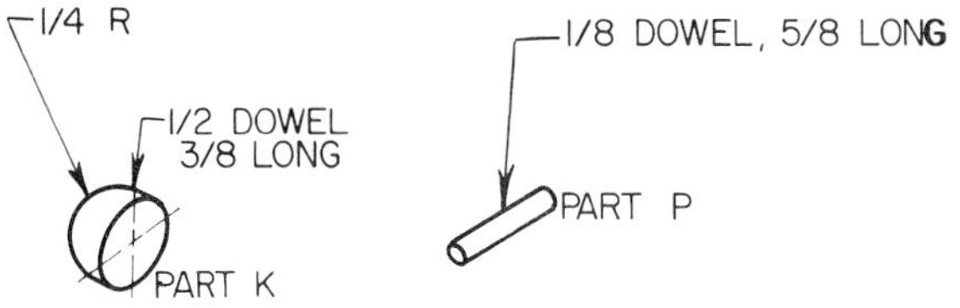

Illus. 47. Parts K and P.

Pickup Truck

Illus. 48. See page E of the color section for a look at the pickup truck in full color.

Key to Assembly Shown in Illus. 50

LETTER	NUMBER REQUIRED	PART	SIZE
A	1	Body	$9\frac{1}{4} \times 4 \times 2\frac{13}{16}''$
B	4	Wheel	$2\frac{1}{4} \times 2\frac{1}{4} \times \frac{3}{4}''$
C	1	Spare tire	$2\frac{1}{4} \times 2\frac{1}{4} \times \frac{7}{16}''$
D	5	Hub	$\frac{1}{2}''$ dowel, $\frac{1}{2}''$ long
E	2	Headlight	$\frac{1}{2}''$ dowel, $\frac{5}{16}''$ long
F	1	Front bumper	$4 \times \frac{7}{8} \times \frac{1}{2}''$
G	1	Back bumper	$4 \times 1 \times \frac{1}{2}''$
H	2	Front fender	$5 \times 2\frac{1}{4} \times \frac{3}{4}''$
I	2	Running board	$2\frac{3}{8} \times \frac{3}{4} \times \frac{5}{16}''$
J	2	Rear fender	$4 \times 3 \times \frac{3}{4}''$
K	2	Bed side	$4\frac{1}{4} \times 1\frac{1}{8} \times \frac{5}{16}''$
L	1	Bed end	$2\frac{1}{2} \times 1\frac{1}{8} \times \frac{5}{16}''$
M	1	Bed bottom	$4\frac{1}{4} \times 3\frac{1}{8} \times \frac{5}{16}''$
N	1	Tailgate	$2\frac{5}{16} \times 1\frac{1}{8} \times \frac{5}{16}''$
O	1	Spacer	$3\frac{3}{4} \times 1\frac{3}{4} \times \frac{1}{8}''$
P	1	Front axle	$\frac{1}{4}''$ dowel, $3\frac{1}{2}''$ long
Q	1	Back axle	$\frac{1}{4}''$ dowel, $3\frac{7}{8}''$ long
R	1	Radiator cap	$\frac{1}{8}''$ dowel, $\frac{1}{2}''$ long
S	1	Tire support	$\frac{1}{4}''$ dowel, $1''$ long

TOOLS AND SUPPLIES

Jointer   *Drill press*
Table saw   *Band saw*
Hammer   *Nail set*
Twist bit   *Hole saw*
Router   *Wire brads*
Straight-cutting   *No. 6 finishing nails*
*   router bit*   *Belt sander*
Glue

CONSTRUCTION NOTES

Part A (Illus. 49)

Obtain a piece of stock large enough for part A (body). The stock may have to be laminated, depending upon the stock size you decide to use. Lay out the shape of the side and, using a router with a straight-cutting bit, cut out the window on both sides. Drill the holes for parts P and Q (axles). (See Illus. 54 and 55 for parts P and Q.)

With the band saw, cut out the shape of the truck as seen from the side; then cut out the shape as seen from the top. Drill out the hole for part R (radiator cap). (See Illus. 53 for part R.) Sand this part before continuing.

Parts K, L, M, N, and O (Illus. 51)

Start these parts by planing enough lumber to the correct thickness with a

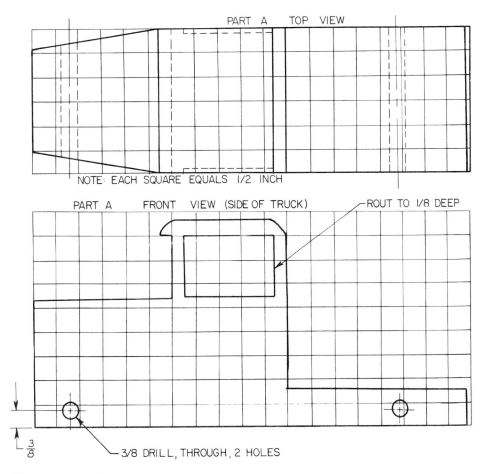

Illus. 49. Part A.

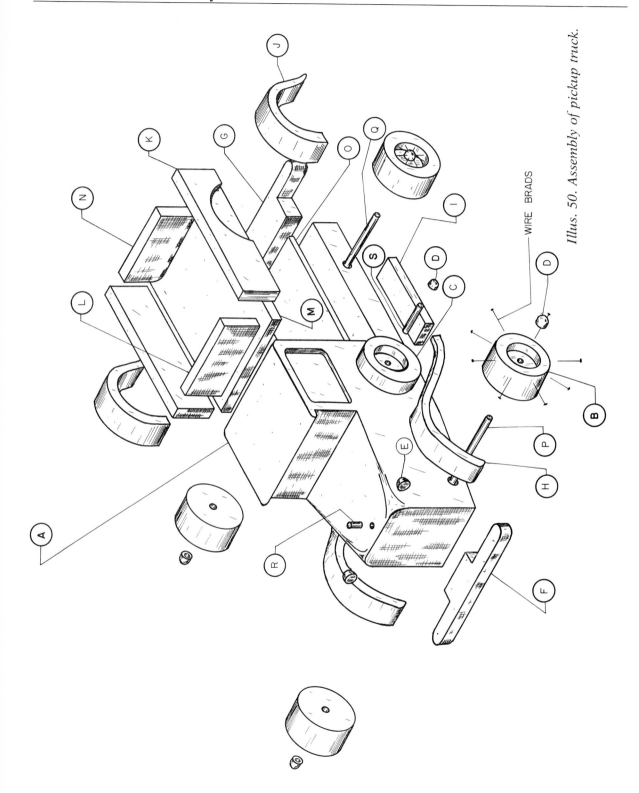

WIRE BRADS

Illus. 50. Assembly of pickup truck.

jointer or planer. Remember to use a long board on the jointer; this ensures a safer operation. It is much better to waste a little wood than to take a chance of losing a finger or a hand.

These parts can be cut to size with a table saw or a radial arm saw. Since they are very small, for safety reasons use a push stick when using the table saw. If using a radial arm saw, hold small parts against the fence with a scrap board.

Parts K, L, and M (bed side, bed end, and bed bottom) can be glued together at this point. Once these dry, use two small nails to attach part N (tailgate). Put the nails at the bottom of part N so that it will swivel open. Resaw or joint a board to the correct thickness for part O (spacer), then cut it to size. Part N, which has been assembled, can be glued to part O; part O can be glued to part A.

Parts F and G (Illus. 52)

Parts F and G (bumpers) should be cut out with a band saw. Sand and attach each bumper to the body with glue and two No. 6 finishing nails. Predrill holes for the nails to prevent them from splitting. The bumper's bottom should be flush with the bottom of part A.

Parts R and E (Illus. 53)

Cut part R (radiator cap) from a dowel rod. Glue part R into part A so that it protrudes out of part A by approximately ⅛ inch. Part E (headlights) should be made from a ½-inch dowel that's 3 inches long or slightly longer. Sand the ends of the dowel round with a belt sander, then finish rounding by hand. Once the headlights are made, cut them to the correct length. Predrill holes and use a fourpenny nail to attach the headlight to the body approximately ½ inch below the hood surface on the side of part A.

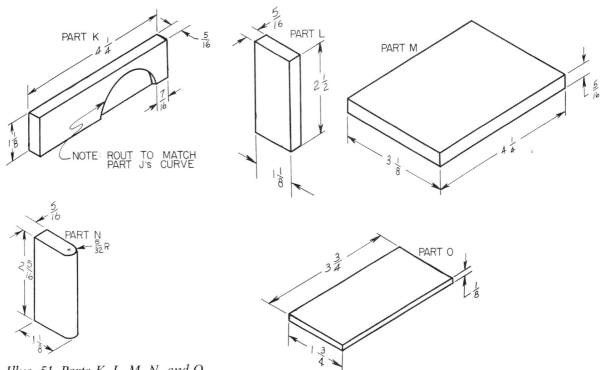

Illus. 51. Parts K, L, M, N, and O.

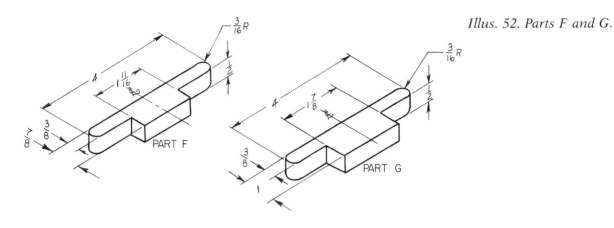

Illus. 52. Parts F and G.

PART F

PART G

Illus. 53. Parts E and R.

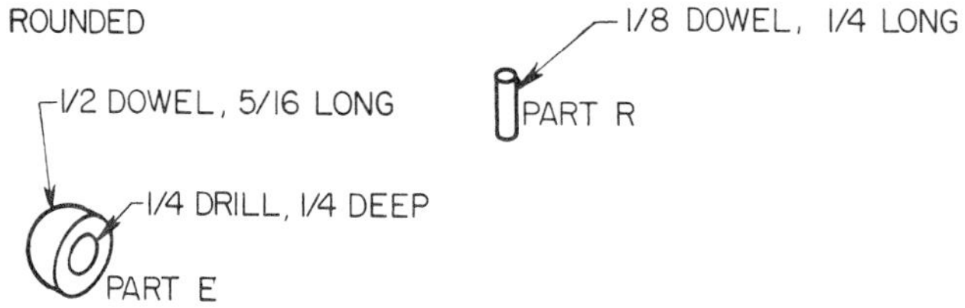

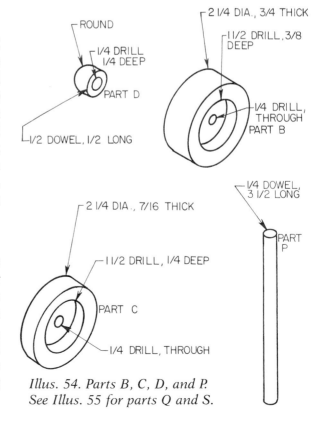

Parts B, C, D, P, Q, and S (Illus. 54 and 55)

The methods for making parts B and C (wheel and spare tire) are detailed on page 45. Once these are made, cut parts P, Q, and S (front axle, back axle, and tire support) to length. Put the axle through the hole in part A and glue on parts B and D (wheel and hub). Make sure the glue does not get inside the hole of part A which, when dried, would prevent the axle from turning. Glue part S into part A and attach part C in the same manner.

Parts H, I, and J (Illus. 56)

Each of these parts can be cut on the band saw. Parts H and J (front and rear fenders) should be made out of birch plywood; this gives the fenders strength and helps prevent breaking. Using a router, rout out the recessed area in part K (bed side), as shown in Illus. 51. Once this is done, glue the fenders and the running board to parts K and A.

Illus. 54. Parts B, C, D, and P.
See Illus. 55 for parts Q and S.

Illus. 55. Parts Q and S.

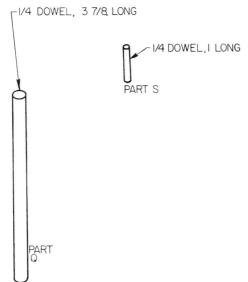

1/4 DOWEL, 3 7/8 LONG

1/4 DOWEL, 1 LONG

PART S

PART Q

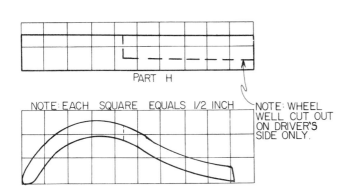

PART H

NOTE: EACH SQUARE EQUALS 1/2 INCH

NOTE: WHEEL WELL CUT OUT ON DRIVER'S SIDE ONLY.

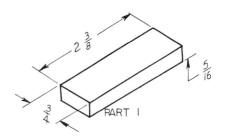

$2\frac{3}{8}$

$\frac{5}{16}$

$\frac{3}{4}$

PART I

NOTE: EACH SQUARE EQUALS 1/2 INCH

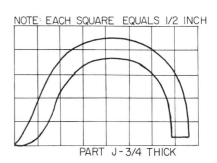

PART J - 3/4 THICK

Illus. 56. Parts H, I, and J.

MG (Sports Car)

Illus. 57. See page D of the color section for a look at the MG in full color.

Key to Assembly Shown in Illus. 59

LETTER	NUMBER REQUIRED	PART	SIZE
A	1	Body	$10 \times 3^{1}/_{4} \times 2^{3}/_{4}''$
B	1	Radiator Cap	$^{1}/_{4}''$ dowel, $^{3}/_{4}''$ long
C	1	Windshield	$2^{11}/_{16} \times 1^{3}/_{8} \times ^{3}/_{32}''$ plastic
D	1	Dashboard	$2^{1}/_{4} \times ^{3}/_{4} \times ^{3}/_{16}''$
E	1	Steering wheel	$1^{3}/_{8}''$ round moulding, $^{3}/_{16}''$ long
F	1	Steering wheel shaft	$^{1}/_{4}''$ dowel, $1''$ long
G	1	Convertible top	$2^{5}/_{8} \times 2 \times ^{1}/_{2}''$
H	2	Front fender	$7^{1}/_{4} \times 2^{1}/_{2} \times ^{3}/_{4}''$
I	2	Back fender	$3^{3}/_{4} \times 2^{1}/_{2} \times ^{3}/_{4}''$
J	1	Front bumper	$3^{1}/_{4} \times 1 \times ^{3}/_{8}''$
K	2	Headlight	$^{1}/_{4}''$ dowel, $^{3}/_{8}''$ long
L	2	Headlight support	$^{1}/_{4}''$ dowel, $^{1}/_{2}''$ long
M	5	Wheel	$2^{1}/_{4}''$ diameter $\times ^{3}/_{4}''$ thick
N	4	Hubcap	$^{1}/_{2}''$ dowel, $^{1}/_{2}''$ long
O	1	Back bumper	$4^{1}/_{2} \times ^{3}/_{4} \times ^{3}/_{8}''$
P	1	Back axle	$^{1}/_{4}''$ dowel, $4^{5}/_{8}''$ long
Q	1	Front axle	$^{1}/_{4}''$ dowel, $3^{3}/_{8}''$ long
R	2	Tailpipe	$^{1}/_{4}''$ dowel, $1''$ long
S	1	Spare tire support	$^{1}/_{4}''$ dowel, $1''$ long

pipe). (See Illus. 60 for parts P and Q, Illus. 63 for parts B and L, Illus. 64 for part F, and Illus. 65 for part R.)

Parts M, N, P, Q, and S (Illus. 60)

Cut the dowels for parts P and Q (axles); note that they are different in length. Use a drill press and hole saw to make the four wheels. Cut the recess out with a drill press and a Forstner bit. Use a dowel rod to make part N (hubcap). Sand the ends round with a belt or disc sander and finish sanding by hand. Hold part N in a hand-screw clamp and drill the required hole with a twist bit and drill press. Glue part M (wheel) onto the dowel for either part P or Q. With the dowel protruding through the wheel by ¼ inch, glue part N onto the dowel. Once these parts have dried, drill the holes for the wire brads with an electric hand drill and a ¹⁄₁₆-inch twist bit. Very carefully, drive the wire brads through part M (wheel) and into part N (hubcap). Counter-sink the wire brads with a nail set. Mount the spare tire to the back of part A by drilling a hole into part A and gluing part S (spare tire support) into part A. Make sure the spokes are on the spare tire before it is glued into part A.

Parts H and I (Illus. 61)

Parts H and I (fenders) can both be cut out with a jigsaw or a band saw. They should be glued to the body so that they are approximately ¼ inch above the wheels.

Parts J and O (Illus. 62)

Plane a piece of stock to the correct thickness for parts J and O (bumpers) with a jointer or planer. Cut parts J and O out with either a jigsaw or band saw. They should be nailed with No. 4 finishing nails and glued to part A (body). The bottoms of parts J and O should be flush with the bottom of part A. Countersink and fill the nail holes.

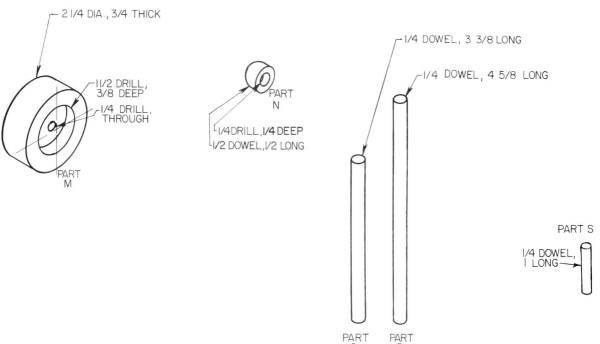

Illus. 60. Parts M, N, P, Q, and S.

NOTE: EACH SQUARE EQUALS 1/2 INCH   PART H - 3/4 THICK

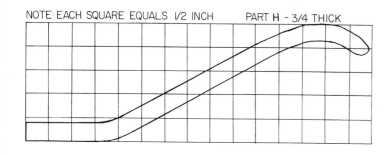

PART I - 3/4 THICK

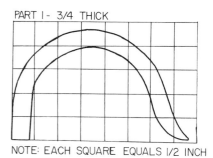

NOTE: EACH SQUARE EQUALS 1/2 INCH

Illus. 61. Parts H and I.

PART J - 1/2 THICK

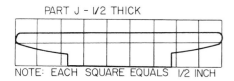

NOTE: EACH SQUARE EQUALS 1/2 INCH

PART O - 3/8 THICK

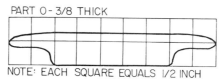

NOTE: EACH SQUARE EQUALS 1/2 INCH

Illus. 62. Parts J and O.

Parts B, K, and L (Illus. 63)

Cut parts B (radiator cap) and L (headlight support) to length. Use a long dowel rod and sand the cone shape on part K (headlight) on each end of the dowel rod. Cut part K from the long dowel rod. Drill the hole in part K for part L to fit into. Glue part B into part A so that part B protrudes out by 1/8 of an inch. Glue part L into part A so that part L protrudes out by 1/4 of an inch. Glue part K onto part L so that part K touches part A (body).

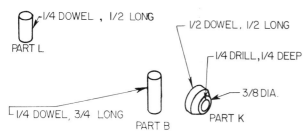

1/4 DOWEL , 1/2 LONG
PART L
1/2 DOWEL, 1/2 LONG
1/4 DRILL, 1/4 DEEP
3/8 DIA.
1/4 DOWEL, 3/4 LONG
PART B
PART K

Illus. 63. Parts B, K, and L.

Parts C, D, E, and F (Illus. 64)

The plastic used for part C (windshield) can be cut on a band saw or jigsaw with a very fine-toothed blade. The edges may have to be filed, sanded, and buffed. Once this piece is made, gently tap it into the groove in part A (body). Place a small block of wood under part A so that the body rests on the wood and not the wheels. Tapping directly on part A when it is resting on the wheels can break an axle. Part C should fit firmly in the saw kerf in part A and should not require nails or glue. Part F (steering wheel shaft) should be cut and glued into part A so that it protrudes out of part A by approximately 3/4 of an inch.

Next, cut part E from a piece of round moulding. Drill the hole on a drill press using a twist bit. Glue part E (steering wheel) onto part F so that they are flush on the outside or the driver's side. Part D (dashboard) can be cut from a thin piece of stock on a jigsaw or a band saw. Round the contours with a wood rasp and file, and by hand sanding.

Glue part D onto part A.

Parts G and R (Illus. 65)

Part G (convertible top) should be sanded on a belt sander to the shape shown in Illus. 65. To prevent injuries to your fingers, use a hand-screw clamp to hold part

Train.

Piper Cub.

Biplane.

Helicopter.

Piper Cub with pontoons.

MG.

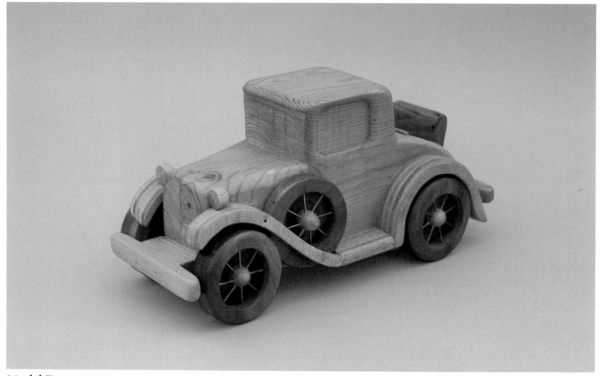

Model T coupé.

Pickup truck.

Model T sedan.

F

Iron.

Toaster.

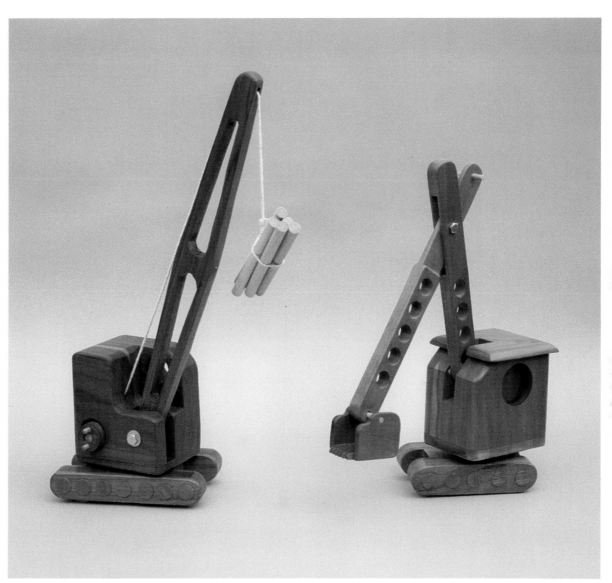

Crane and steam shovel.

Eighteen wheeler.

Eighteen wheeler with tractor and trailer detached.

G while it is being sanded. Glue part G to part A (body). Cut part R (tailpipe) and glue it into part A so that it protrudes out of part A by approximately ⅜ of an inch.

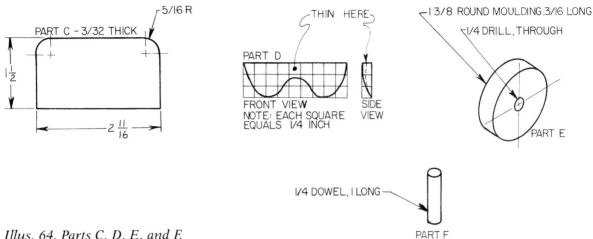

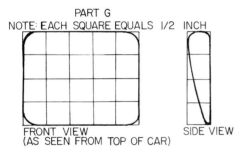

Illus. 64. Parts C, D, E, and F.

PART G
NOTE: EACH SQUARE EQUALS 1/2 INCH

FRONT VIEW
(AS SEEN FROM TOP OF CAR)

SIDE VIEW

Illus. 65. Parts G and R.

Model T Coupé

Illus. 66. See page D of the color section for a look at the Model T coupé in full color.

Key to Assembly Shown in Illus. 68

LETTER	NUMBER REQUIRED	PART	SIZE
A	1	Body	$9 \times 4\frac{1}{4} \times 3''$
B	2	Front fender	$\frac{3}{4} \times 1\frac{1}{2} \times 5''$
C	2	Back fender	$\frac{3}{4} \times 2\frac{1}{2} \times 4''$
D	2	Running board	$\frac{3}{4} \times \frac{1}{4} \times 1\frac{3}{4}''$
E	1	Rumble seat	$1\frac{1}{2} \times 1\frac{5}{8} \times 1\frac{15}{16}''$
F	1	Back bumper	$\frac{9}{16} \times \frac{1}{2} \times 4''$
G	1	Front bumper	$1 \times \frac{1}{2} \times 4''$
H	4	Wheel	$2\frac{1}{2} \times 2\frac{1}{2} \times \frac{3}{4}''$
I	1	Spare tire	$2\frac{1}{2} \times 2\frac{1}{2} \times \frac{1}{2}''$
J	4	Hub	$\frac{1}{2}''$ dowel, $\frac{1}{2}''$ long
K	1	Spare hub	$\frac{1}{2}''$ dowel, $\frac{3}{8}''$ long
L	2	Headlight	$\frac{1}{2}''$ dowel, $\frac{3}{8}''$ long
M	1	Rear axle	$\frac{1}{4}''$ dowel, $3\frac{3}{4}''$ long
N	1	Front axle	$\frac{1}{4}''$ dowel, $3\frac{3}{8}''$ long
O	1	Spare tire rod	$\frac{1}{4}''$ dowel, $1''$ long
P	1	Radiator cap	$\frac{1}{8}''$ dowel, $\frac{5}{8}''$ long

TOOLS AND SUPPLIES

Table saw
Drill press
Hole saw
Forstner bit
Try square
Nail set
Wire brads
Wood chisel
Band saw

Router
Disc or belt sander
Twist bit
Ruler
No. 6 finishing nails
Router
Straight-cutting
    router bit

CONSTRUCTION NOTES

Part A (Illus. 67)

Laminate enough stock for part A (body). Lay out the side shape from the side, including the window. First drill the hole for part N (front axle) to fit in. (See Illus. 69 for part N.) Using a router, rout out the window with a straight-cutting bit. Using a band saw, cut the side shape out. Drill the hole for part P (radiator cap). (See Illus. 73 for part P.)

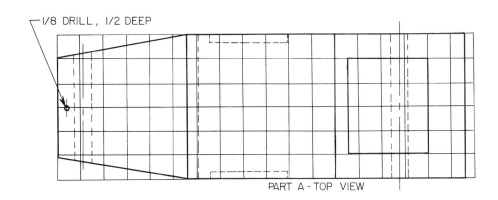

1/8 DRILL, 1/2 DEEP

PART A - TOP VIEW

NOTE: EACH SQUARE EQUALS 1/2 INCH

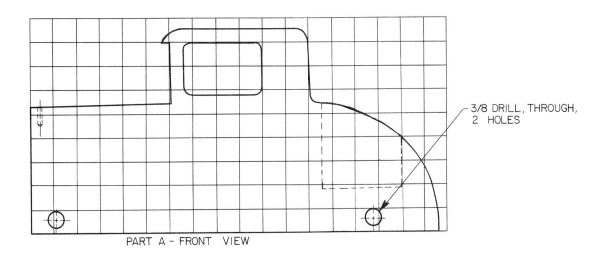

3/8 DRILL, THROUGH, 2 HOLES

PART A - FRONT VIEW

NOTE: NOTCH OUT 1/2 DEEP FOR WHEEL WELL. SEE PHOTO

Illus. 67. Part A.

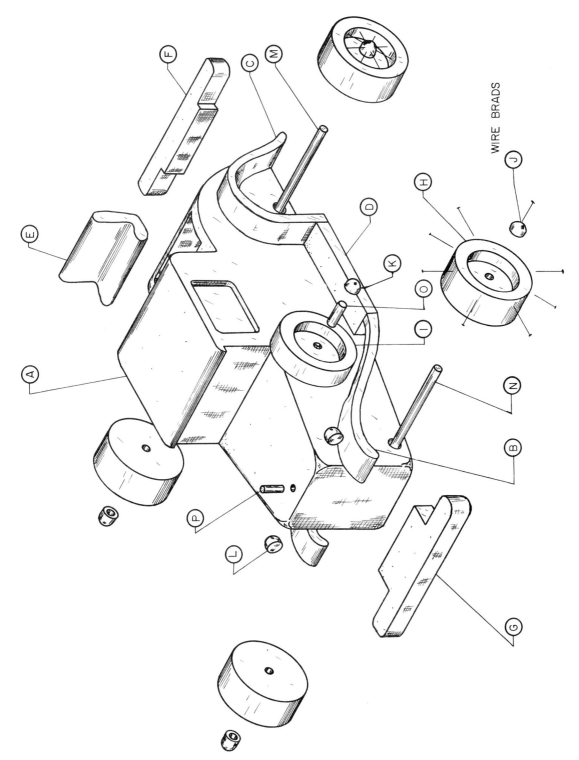

WIRE BRADS

Illus. 68. Assembly of Model T coupé.

Cut out the top-view shape of part A with a band saw. Use a drill press and Forstner bit to drill out the section for part E (rumble seat) to fit into. (See Illus. 73 for part E.) Use a sharp wood chisel to square off the corners.

Parts H, J, M, and N (Illus. 69)

Cut the dowel rods to length for parts M and N (rear and front axles). See page 45 for detailed instructions on making parts H and J (wheels and hubs). Once these parts are made, place the axles in the holes in part A and attach the wire wheels to the axles.

Parts B, C, and D (Illus. 70)

Using a band saw, cut parts B, C, and D (fenders and running board) to their correct shapes. Parts B and C will be stronger if they are made from birch plywood instead of solid stock. Cut out the section for part I (spare tire) with a coping saw. (See Illus. 71 for part I.) Glue part D (running board) to part A so that they are flush on the bottom. Glue parts B and C so that they clear the wheels by approximately ⅛ inch.

Parts I, K, and O (Illus. 71)

Parts I and K (spare tire and spare hub) should be made the same way parts H and

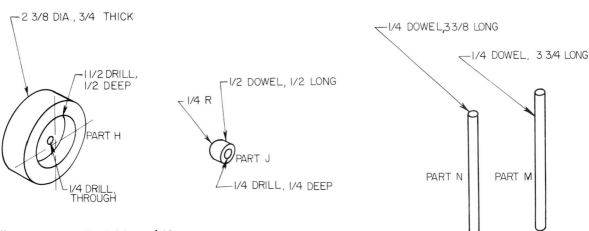

Illus. 69. Parts H, J, M, and N.

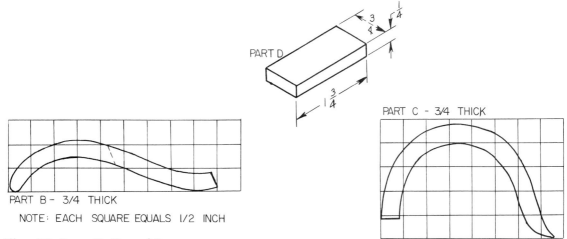

Illus. 70. Parts B, C, and D.

J (wheels and hubs) were made. Part O (spare tire rod) should be made the same way part N was made. (See page 69.) Once these parts are made, assemble them onto part A. Rotate part I, drill the holes for the wire brads, and drive the wire brads into the wheel and hub. Glue part I to part A.

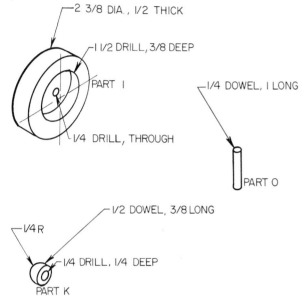

Illus. 71. Parts I, K, and O.

Parts F and G (Illus. 72)

Plane enough stock to the correct thickness for parts F and G (back and front bumpers). Remember to do this on a board longer than necessary to ensure a safe operation. Cut the shape out with a band saw.

Attach parts F and G to part A so that they are flush on the bottoms. Glue and place two No. 6 finishing nails through each bumper. Predrill holes for the nails, set the nails with a nail set, and fill the hole.

Parts E, L, and P (Illus. 73)

Cut part E (rumble seat) out with a band saw. It should be glued into the mortised hole in part A. Cut the dowel rod for part P (radiator cap) to length and glue it into the hole in part A. The radiator cap should protrude out of part A by ⅛ inch.

For part L (headlights), file or sand with a disc or belt sander two ends of a dowel rod so that they are round. Cut them to length and sand the flat sections smooth. Using a ⅟₁₆-inch twist bit, drill a hole through part L into part A. Attach part L to the body by nailing it to part A. Countersink the nails and fill the holes.

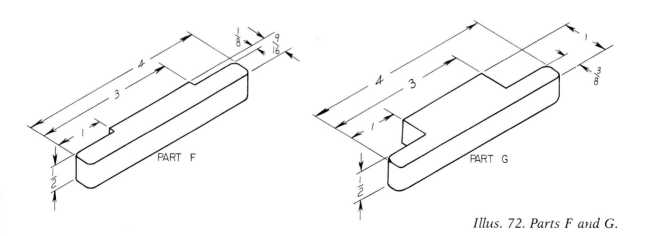

Illus. 72. Parts F and G.

PART E

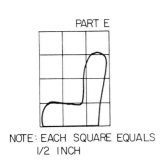

NOTE: EACH SQUARE EQUALS
1/2 INCH

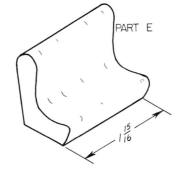

PART E

$1\frac{15}{16}$

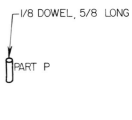

1/8 DOWEL, 5/8 LONG

PART P

1/2 DOWEL
3/8 LONG

PART L

Illus. 73. Parts E, L, and P.

Eighteen Wheeler

Illus. 74. See page H of the color section for a look at the eighteen wheeler in full color.

Key to Assembly Shown in Illus. 75 and 76

LETTER	NUMBER REQUIRED	PART	SIZE
A	1	Frame	$12 \times 2^{3}/_{4} \times {}^{3}/_{4}$" cherry
B	1	Cab	$4^{1}/_{2} \times 2^{3}/_{4} \times 3$" cherry
C	1	Sleeper	$1^{7}/_{8} \times 3^{11}/_{16} \times {}^{7}/_{8}$" cherry
D	1	Grill	$3^{1}/_{2} \times 1^{3}/_{4} \times {}^{1}/_{4}$" walnut
E	1	Front bumper	$3^{1}/_{2} \times {}^{1}/_{2} \times {}^{1}/_{2}$" walnut
F	2	Step	$1 \times {}^{3}/_{4} \times {}^{3}/_{4}$" walnut
G	2	Fender	$2^{3}/_{4} \times 2 \times {}^{3}/_{4}$" cherry
H	2	Gas tank	$1^{1}/_{16} \times 1^{1}/_{16} \times 2^{1}/_{4}$" maple and walnut
I	1	Air foil	$2^{1}/_{4} \times 1^{1}/_{2} \times {}^{5}/_{16}$" walnut
J	2	Air foil support rods	${}^{1}/_{4}$" dowel $\times 1^{1}/_{4}$" long birch
K	2	Muffler	${}^{1}/_{2}$" dowel $\times 2$" long birch
L	2	Exhaust stack	${}^{1}/_{4}$" dowel $\times 1^{3}/_{4}$" long birch
M	2	Lower exhaust pipe	${}^{1}/_{4}$" dowel $\times 2$" long birch
N	4	Headlight	${}^{1}/_{4}$" dowel $\times {}^{5}/_{16}$" long birch
O	1	Trailer hitch	$2 \times 1^{3}/_{4} \times {}^{9}/_{16}$" cherry

P	1	Air filter	$1/2$" dowel × $13/16$" long birch
Q	1	Air filter	$3/8$" dowel × $1/2$" long birch
R	8	Wheel	$1 3/4 × 1 3/4 × 1/2$" walnut
S	10	Rim	$1 × 1 × 1/4$" maple
T	80	Lug nut	$1/8$" dowel, $3/8$" long birch
U	2	Back trailer axle	$1/4$" dowel, $3 3/4$" long birch
V	2	Front wheel	$1 3/4 × 1 3/4 × 3/4$" walnut
W	1	Front tractor axle	$1/4$" dowel, $3/8$" long birch
X	2	Trailer axle	$1/4$" dowel, $3 5/8$" long birch
Y	1	Axle housing	$1 7/8 × 1 3/8 × 4$" cherry
Z	1	Auxiliary wheel housing	$2 1/4 × 1 1/4 × 3/4$" cherry
AA	1	Brace	$2 1/8 × 1 5/8 × 3/4$" cherry
BB	1	Axle	$1/4$" dowel, $2 1/8$" long birch
CC	2	Auxiliary wheel	$1 × 1 × 3/8$" cherry
DD	1	Axle	$1/4$" dowel, $3 1/8$" long birch
EE	1	Hitch	$1/4$" dowel, $1 1/2$" long birch
FF	2	Trailer side	$15 1/2 × 4 × 1/2$" cherry
GG	1	Trailer end	$3 3/8 × 3 × 1/2$" cherry
HH	2	Trailer door	$2 15/16 × 1 9/16 × 1/2$" cherry
II	4	Door pivot rod	$1/8$" dowel, $15/16$" long birch
JJ	4	Horizontal trim	$15 1/2 × 1/4 × 1/8$" walnut
KK	22	Vertical trim	$3 1/2 × 1/4 × 1/8$" walnut
LL	152	Rivet	$1/8$" dowel, $1/4$" long birch
MM	8	Inner wheel	$1 3/4 × 1 3/4 × 1/2$" walnut
NN	1	Trailer bottom	$15 1/2 × 3 3/8 × 1/2$" cherry
OO	1	Trailer top	$15 1/2 × 3 3/8 × 1/2$" cherry

TOOLS AND SUPPLIES

Table saw
Drill press
Band saw
Ruler
Try square
Screwdriver
Wood file
Hole saw
Forstner bit
$3/8$" plug cutter
Nail set
Wood filler
Wire brads
Glue

Wood lathe
Radial arm saw
Coping saw
Pencil
Hand-screw clamp
C-clamp
Belt sander
Twist bit
Woodburning tool
$1 1/4$" × No. 10
   combination drill
   and countersink
Sandpaper
$1 1/4$" × No. 10 flathead
   wood screws

CONSTRUCTION NOTES

Parts A and B (Illus. 77)

Part A (frame) should be cut out with a jigsaw or a band saw. Drill the holes for parts U and W (axles) with a twist bit and drill press. (See Illus. 81 for parts U and W.) Also drill the hole in which will be fitted part EE (hitch), which is part of the trailer. (See Illus. 87 for part EE.) Cut out the side and top shapes of part B (cab) with a band saw.

Glue parts A and B together. Once they have dried, sand them so that they appear to be one solid piece of wood. Lay out the lines for the doors and windows and the three lines on the hood. Using a woodburn-

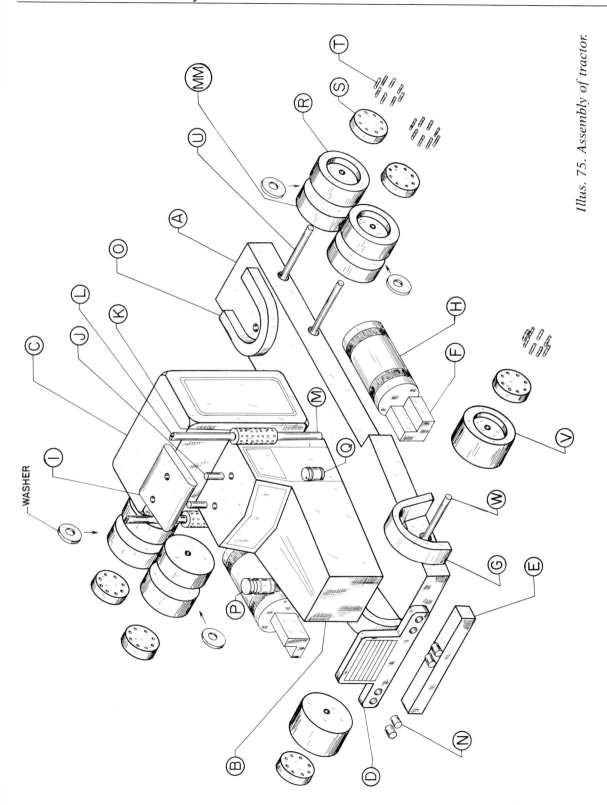

WASHER

Illus. 75. Assembly of tractor.

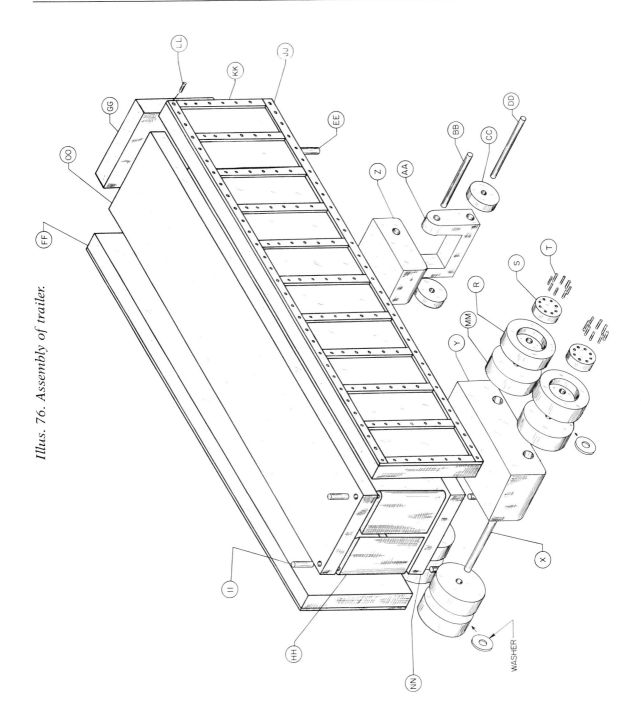

Illus. 76. Assembly of trailer.

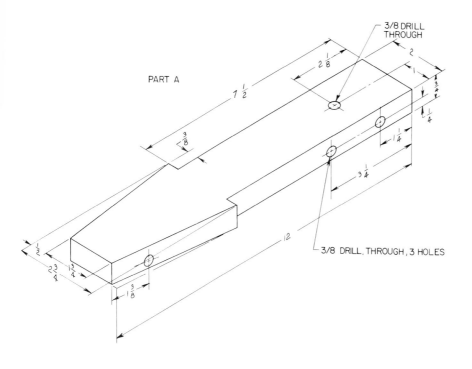

PART A

3/8 DRILL THROUGH

3/8 DRILL, THROUGH, 3 HOLES

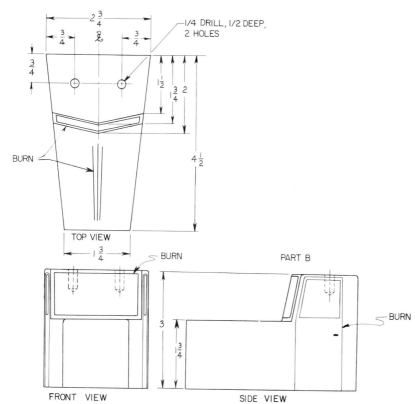

1/4 DRILL, 1/2 DEEP, 2 HOLES

BURN

TOP VIEW

BURN

FRONT VIEW

PART B

BURN

SIDE VIEW

Illus. 77. Parts A and B.

ing tool, burn the outlines for the doors, windows, and hood.

At this point, also make and assemble parts R (wheel), S (rim), T (lug nut), and MM (inner wheel). (See Illus. 81 for a look at these parts.)

Part C (Illus. 78)

Cut part C (sleeper) out with a table saw. Round the edges with a file, belt sander, or disc sander. Lay out the lines and use a woodburning tool to outline the doors on the side of the sleeper. Attach the sleeper to part A (frame) with two 1¼″ × No. 10 flathead wood screws from the bottom of part A. These screws will have to be pre-drilled.

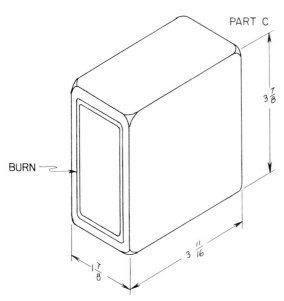

Illus. 78. Part C.

Parts D, E, N, and O (Illus. 79)

Plane a piece of stock that is longer than necessary to the required thickness for part D (grill). Cut this part out on a jigsaw or a band saw. Drill the holes for part N (headlight) with a twist bit and drill press. Use a woodburning tool to burn the design out on the grill. Glue part N (headlight) into part D (grill) so that the parts are flush on each side. Glue part D to part B (cab) and secure it by using two 1-inch wire brads.

Part E (front bumper) can be cut out with the table saw or radial arm saw. Using two 1-inch wire brads, glue and nail part E to part A (frame). Parts E and A should be flush on the bottom.

Part O (trailer hitch) should be cut out with a band saw or jigsaw. Glue it to part A.

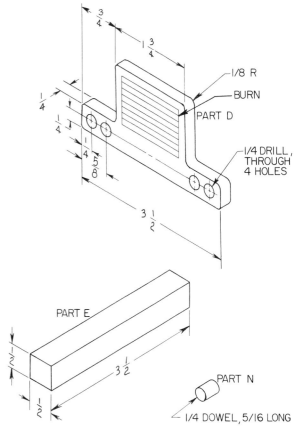

Illus. 79. Parts D, E, N, and O.

Parts I, J, K, L, and M (Illus. 80)

Cut part I (air foil) out with either a table saw or radial arm saw. Use a larger board than necessary to ensure a safer operation. Drill the holes through part I and into part B (cab). (See Illus. 77 for part B.) Cut part J (air foil support) to length. Glue part J into part I, then sand parts I and J flush on top. Glue part J into part B so that there is approximately ⅜ of an inch between part I and part B at the dowel's center.

From a dowel rod, cut parts L (exhaust stack) and M (lower exhaust pipe) to length. Drill the holes in the top of part L and sand the angle on a disc or belt sander. Cut part K (muffler) to length and lay out the holes. Use a V-block to hold part K, and drill the holes on the side of part K with a drill press. (See page 37 for instructions on how to use a V-block.) Also drill the holes in the top and bottom of part K with a drill press and a twist bit.

Glue parts L and M into part K, as shown in Illus. 75. Using two 1-inch wire brads, nail part K to part C (sleeper). Drive the brads through the small holes in part K so that they will not be noticed; use a nail set to countersink them.

Parts R, S, T, U, V, W, and MM (Illus. 81)

Cut parts U and W (axles) to their correct length. From a ¾-inch piece of stock, use a

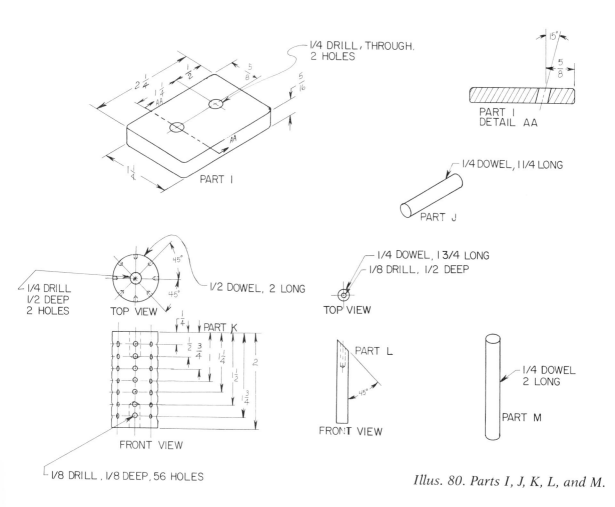

Illus. 80. Parts I, J, K, L, and M.

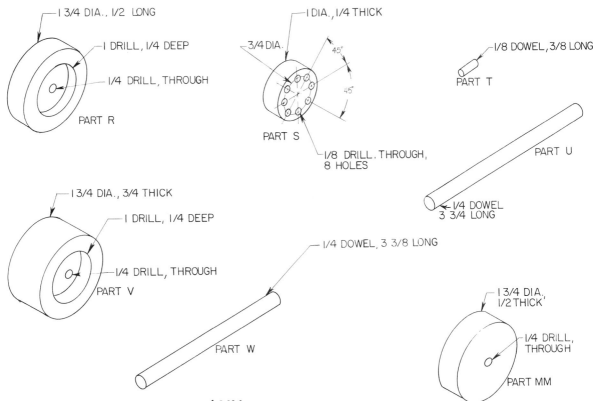

Illus. 81. Parts R, S, T, U, V, W, and MM.

hole saw to cut out part V (front wheel). Drill the recess with a Forstner bit and drill press. Using a ½-inch-thick piece of stock, use the same procedure to cut out part R (wheel). Part S (rim) should be cut out with a jigsaw and glued into the recessed portion of parts R and V. Sand parts R and S and parts V and S so that they are flush on the outside.

Lay out the holes for part T to fit into, and drill these holes on the drill press with a twist bit. Cut part T (lug nuts), sand one end, and glue the rough end into part S so that part T protrudes out of part S by ¹⁄₁₆ to ⅛ of an inch.

Use a hole saw and a drill press to make part MM (inner wheel). Slide parts W (front tractor axle) and U (back tractor axle) into the holes in part A (frame). Glue part V to part W. Put part U through the hole in part A and glue part MM on first.

Then place a small washer on the axle (which acts as a spacer) and glue on part R (wheel). The extra wheels you have made will be used for the trailer, which is described on pages 80–83.

Parts F, G, H, P, and Q (Illus. 82)

Cut out part G (fender) with a jigsaw or a band saw. Glue part G to part A, making sure the front wheel does not rub against the fender. Leave about ¼ inch between the wheel and the fender.

Part F (step) can be cut from a square board that has a rabbet joint cut in it. This board should be longer than necessary to ensure a safe operation. Glue part F onto part A so that the bottom of parts F and A are flush.

Part H (gas tank) should be glued up, then turned on a wood lathe. Make this part longer than necessary so that the ends

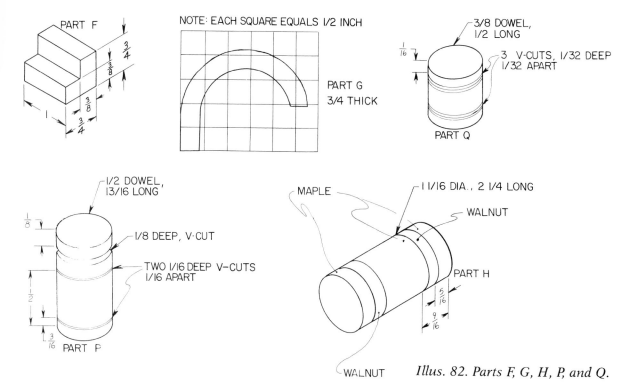

Illus. 82. Parts F, G, H, P, and Q.

can be cut off and sanded smooth. Doing this will eliminate showing where the drive center and the cup center were. Sand part H while it is on the lathe. Attach part H to part C (sleeper) with 1¼″ × No. 10 flathead wood screws through the bottom of part H and into part C. Use a 1¼″ × No. 10 combination drill and countersink to predrill the holes for these screws.

Parts P and Q (air filters) can be turned on a lathe, again from a piece that is longer than necessary. Once turned, cut them to length and sand the ends flat. Use two 1-inch wire brads to attach parts P and Q to part B (cab). Countersink the holes and fill with wood filler.

Parts FF, GG, NN, and OO (Illus. 83)

All of these parts for the trailer should be made from ½-inch stock. Once the stock has been planed to the correct thickness on a planer or jointer, cut the parts to their correct sizes with a table saw. Glue these parts together as shown in Illus. 76. Cut part GG (trailer end) to fit into the hole at the end of the trailer after part FF (side), NN (bottom), and OO (top) have been glued together. This will ensure a better-fitting end. Glue part GG into the hole in the end of the trailer; then sand all of these parts with a belt sander.

Parts HH and II (Illus. 84)

Cut the dowels for part II (door pivot rod) to length. Part HH (trailer door) can be cut on either a radial arm saw or table saw. Use a longer piece of stock than necessary for this operation. Once the doors are cut to size, sand the bevels and the round corners on them with a belt sander. Drill the holes with a drill press.

Drill the two holes in parts NN and OO (trailer bottom and trailer top). (See Illus. 83 for parts NN and OO.) Glue part II into OO and fit it into the holes on part HH. Part HH should *not* be glued to part II and should be allowed to turn freely.

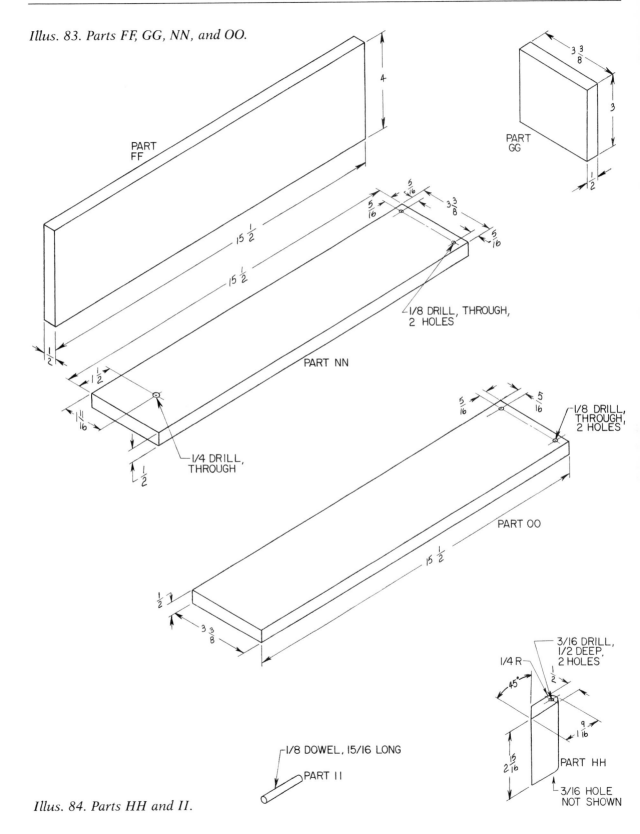

Illus. 83. Parts FF, GG, NN, and OO.

PART
FF

$3\frac{3}{8}$

3

PART
GG

$\frac{1}{2}$

4

$15\frac{1}{2}$

$15\frac{1}{2}$

$\frac{5}{16}$

$\frac{5}{16}$

$3\frac{3}{8}$

$\frac{5}{16}$

1/8 DRILL, THROUGH,
2 HOLES

PART NN

$\frac{1}{2}$

$1\frac{1}{2}$

$1\frac{11}{16}$

1/4 DRILL,
THROUGH

$\frac{1}{2}$

$\frac{5}{16}$

$\frac{5}{16}$

1/8 DRILL,
THROUGH,
2 HOLES

PART OO

$\frac{1}{2}$

$3\frac{3}{8}$

$15\frac{1}{2}$

3/16 DRILL,
1/2 DEEP,
2 HOLES

1/4 R

45°

$\frac{1}{2}$

$1\frac{9}{16}$

$2\frac{15}{16}$

PART HH

3/16 HOLE
NOT SHOWN

1/8 DOWEL, 15/16 LONG

PART II

Illus. 84. Parts HH and II.

Parts JJ, KK, and LL (Illus. 85)

Cut the dowel rods for part LL (rivet) with a pocketknife or a very fine coping-saw blade. Parts JJ and KK (horizontal and vertical trim) should be ripped on a table saw from a piece of stock that has been planed to ¼ inch thick. Cut part JJ to length and glue it on part FF. (See Illus. 83 for part FF.) Cut part KK (vertical trim) to fit and glue it in place as shown in Illus. 76. Lay out the spacing for the holes and drill the small holes with a drill press. Glue part LL into parts JJ and KK so that part LL protrudes by approximately ⅟₁₆ of an inch or less. Using a small block of wood and sandpaper, sand part LL by hand so that it is flush with JJ and KK.

Parts R, S, T, X, Y, and MM (Illus. 86)

Cut part Y (axle housing) out with a radial arm saw or table saw. Round the corners with a band saw and drill the holes for the axles with a twist bit and a drill press. Cut part X (trailer axle) to length. Parts R, S, T, and MM (wheel, rim, lug nut, and inner wheel) should have been made and assembled when the cab was made.

Glue part Y so that it is two inches from the end of part NN (trailer bottom) and is centered from side to side. Slide part X (trailer axle) through the hole in part Y (axle housing). Glue part MM (inner wheel) onto the axle. Slide a washer on the axle to act as a spacer, then glue on part R (wheel).

Parts Z, AA, BB, CC, DD, and EE (Illus. 87)

Part Z (auxiliary wheel housing) can be cut out with a radial arm saw. Round the corners with the band saw and drill the holes with a drill press. Make part CC (auxiliary wheel) with a hole saw.

Cut the dowels to length for parts BB and DD (axles). Part AA (brace) can be cut with a band saw, and the hole drilled with a drill press. Slide part BB through parts AA and Z. Glue should be applied to part AA, but not part Z. The dowel should turn freely inside of part Z. Slide part DD into part AA and glue part CC (wheels) onto part DD. Part DD should turn freely inside of part AA.

Cut the dowel rod for part EE (hitch), and glue it into the hole in part NN so that it is flush on the inside of the trailer and protrudes out on the bottom side of the trailer by approximately 1 inch.

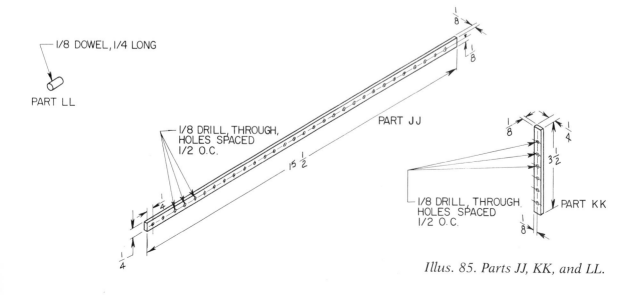

Illus. 85. Parts JJ, KK, and LL.

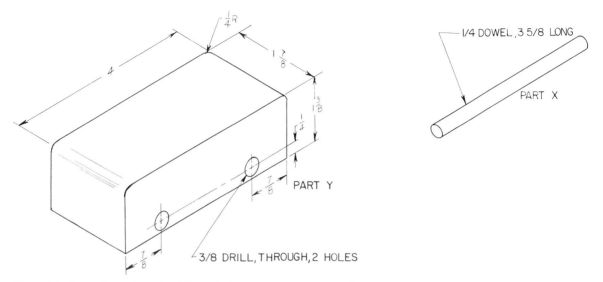

Illus. 86. Parts X and Y. See Illus. 81 for parts R, S, T, and MM.

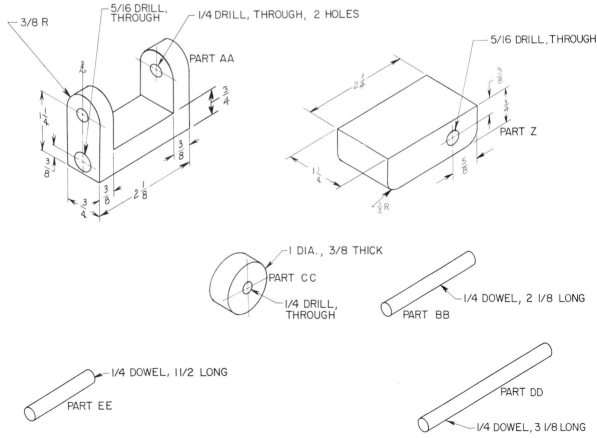

Illus. 87. Parts Z, AA, BB, CC, DD, and EE.

Steam Shovel

Illus. 88. See page G of the color section for a look at the steam shovel in full color.

Key to Assembly Shown in Illus. 90

LETTER	NUMBER REQUIRED	PART	SIZE
A	2	Body	$4^1/_8 \times 5 \times ^3/_4''$
B	2	Body	$4^1/_8 \times 5 \times ^3/_4''$
C	1	Body	$4^1/_8 \times 5 \times ^3/_4''$
D	1	Top	$4^1/_2 \times 4^1/_2 \times ^3/_8''$
E	2	Shovel side	$2^1/_2 \times 2 \times ^1/_4''$
F	1	Shovel bottom	$2^1/_2 \times 1^1/_2 \times ^1/_4''$
G	1	Shovel back	$1^1/_2 \times 1^3/_8 \times ^1/_4''$
H	1	Shovel pivot rod	$^1/_4''$ dowel, 2'' long
I	1	Body bottom	$3^3/_4 \times 5 \times ^1/_2''$
J	1	Track connector	$3^3/_4 \times ^3/_8 \times ^3/_4''$
K	2	Outer track	$6^1/_8 \times 1^1/_2 \times ^1/_4''$
L	2	Inner track	$6^1/_8 \times 1^1/_2 \times ^1/_4''$

M	2	Track center	$6^{1}/_{8} \times 1^{1}/_{2} \times {}^{3}/_{4}"$
N	1	Boom	${}^{3}/_{4} \times 1^{1}/_{4} \times 11"$
O	1	Boom	$13 \times 1^{1}/_{4} \times {}^{3}/_{4}"$
P	1	Post	${}^{1}/_{2}"$ dowel, $2^{1}/_{4}"$ long
Q	1	Spacer	$2 \times 2 \times {}^{3}/_{8}"$
R	1	Lock washer	$1^{1}/_{4} \times 1^{1}/_{4} \times {}^{1}/_{2}"$
S	10	Fake track roller	${}^{3}/_{4} \times {}^{3}/_{4} \times {}^{1}/_{8}"$
T	6	Axle	${}^{1}/_{4}"$ dowel, $1^{1}/_{8}"$ long
U	6	Wheel	$1 \times 1 \times {}^{5}/_{8}"$
V	1	Handle	${}^{1}/_{4}"$ dowel rod, $1^{1}/_{4}"$ long

TOOLS AND SUPPLIES

Jointer	Table saw
Drill press	Hole saw
Band saw	Try square
Hammer	1" bolt with wing nut
3" lag bolt	Twist bit
Forstner bit	Belt sander

CONSTRUCTION NOTES

All the parts on the steam shovel are made of cherry, except part S, which is made of walnut.

Parts A, B, C, and D (Illus. 89 and 91)

Parts A, B, and C (bodies) should be cut on a jigsaw or band saw. Glue these parts together and sand them with a belt sander. Drill the large hole with a Forstner bit, and the small hole with a twist bit and drill press. Part D (top) can also be cut on a band saw. It should be glued to parts A, B, and C.

NOTE: EACH SQUARE EQUALS
1 INCH

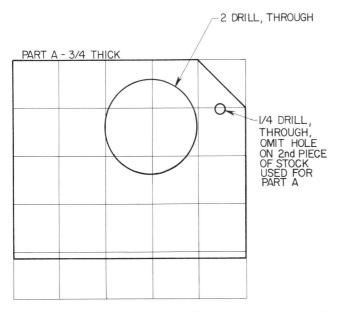

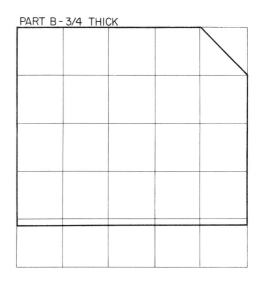

Illus. 89. Parts A and B. See Illus. 91 for parts C and D.

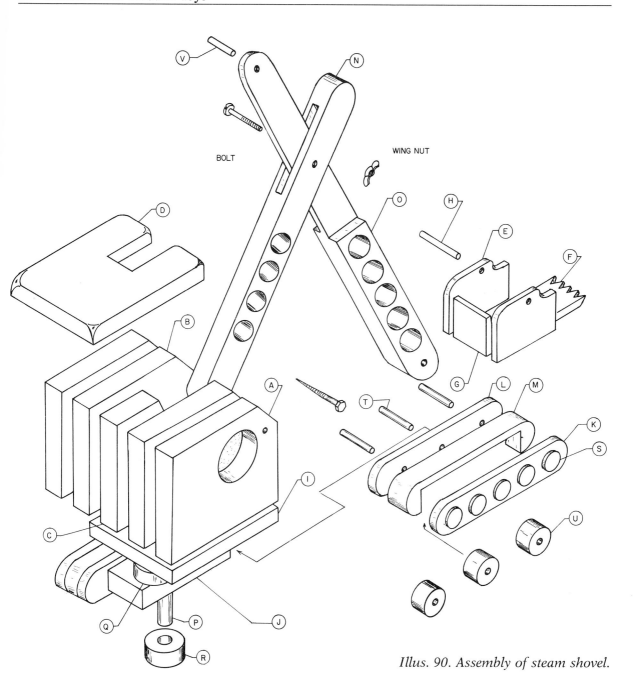

BOLT

WING NUT

Illus. 90. Assembly of steam shovel.

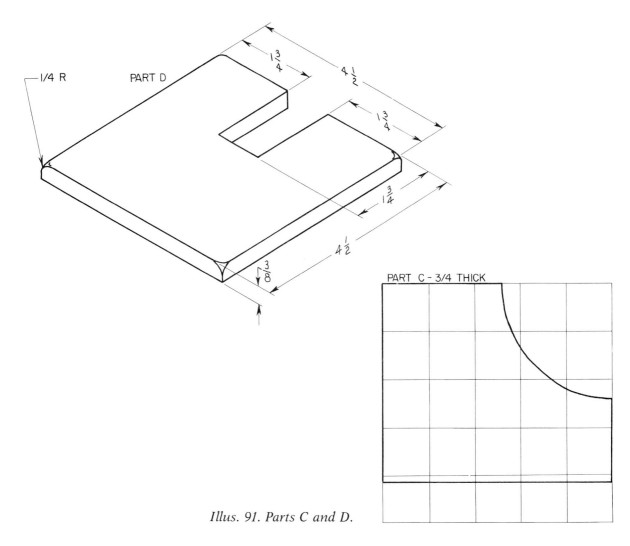

Illus. 91. Parts C and D.

Parts N, O, V (Illus. 92)

Cut parts N and O (boom) out with the table saw; then cut the curves on the band saw. Drill the holes on a drill press with a twist bit and a Forstner bit. See pages 42 and 43 for information on how to cut the mortise.

Once parts N and O are sanded, put part N into the space between parts A and B. Attach part N with a lag bolt, which should make the boom fit firmly. As the child plays with the toy, the boom may become loose; when this happens, tighten the bolt.

Slide part O into the mortise in part N. Drill the hole in part O, making sure part O swivels correctly. Attach parts N and O with a bolt and a wing nut. Cut part V (handle) and glue it into part O so that it is centered on part O.

Parts E, F, G, and H (Illus. 93)

Plane or resaw enough stock for parts E, F, and G (shovel side, shovel bottom, and shovel back). Cut these parts out with a band saw. Glue them as shown in Illus. 90 and drill the hole in parts E and F with a drill press and twist bit. Cut part H (shovel pivot rod) and slide it into parts E, F, and O. Part H should be glued into parts E and F, and should swivel freely on part O.

Illus. 92. Parts N, O, and V.

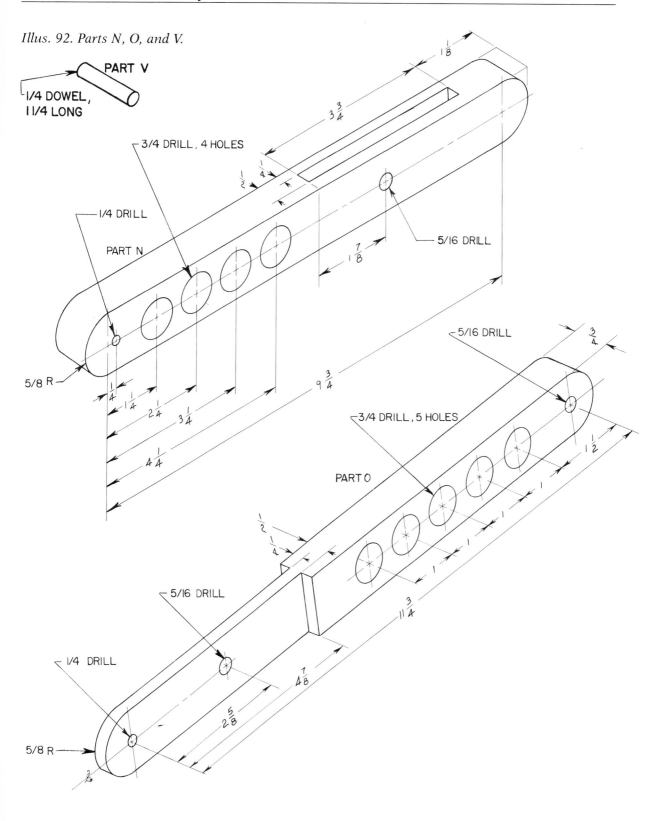

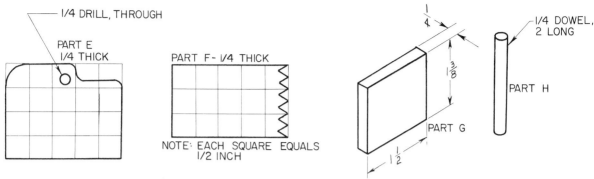

Illus. 93. Parts E, F, G, and H.

Parts K, L, M, S, T, and U (Illus. 94)

Cut part T (axle). Plane or resaw a piece of stock large enough to make parts K and L (outer and inner tracks). Cut parts K, L, and M (track center) out with a band saw. Glue parts K, L, and M so that they are flush on the outside; sand them with a belt sander so that they look like one piece of wood. Drill the required holes through part L and into part K.

Make part U (wheels) on a drill press, using a hole saw. Slide the wheels into the cavity portion of parts K, L, and M and drive part T (axle) through part L, then through part U (wheel), and glue them into part K. Make sure part T (axle) is flush on the outside of part L. See pages 39 and 40 for detailed instructions on making part S (fake track roller). Glue part S to part K (outer track) so that the fake track rollers are equally spaced along part K.

Illus. 94. Parts K, L, M, S, T, and U.

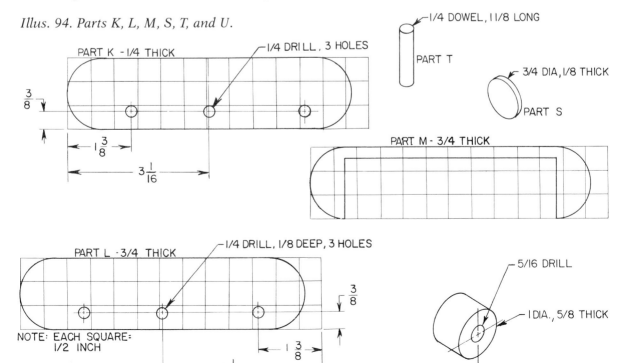

Parts I, J, P, Q, and R (Illus. 95)

Cut both parts I and J (body bottom and track connector) with the table saw. Drill the hole in part J with a drill press and twist bit. Also use the drill press to make parts Q (spacer) and R (lock washer). Drill the centers out on each of these parts to the required size.

Cut part P to length. Glue parts K, L, M, S, T and U to part J, keeping the top of each flush. Part J should be centered on part L from end to end. Glue part I (body bottom) to parts A, B, and C. Part P should be glued into the hole in part I. Slide part Q (spacer) over part P, slide part J onto part P, and finally glue part R (lock washer) to part P. Make sure that part J swivels easily on part P.

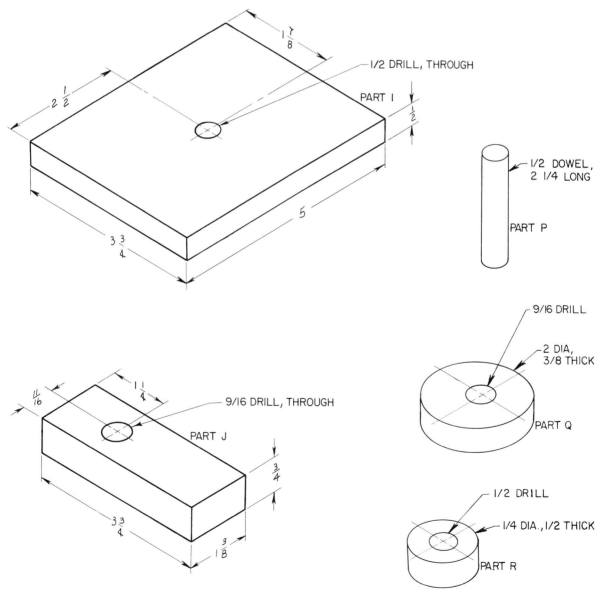

Illus. 95. Parts I, J, P, Q, and R.

Crane

Illus. 96. See page G of the color section for a look at the crane in full color.

Key to Assembly Shown in Illus. 97

LETTER	NUMBER REQUIRED	PART	SIZE
A	1	Body	$1\frac{1}{2} \times 5 \times 5''$
B	1	Body	$\frac{3}{4} \times 5 \times 5''$
C	1	Body	$\frac{3}{4} \times 5 \times 5''$
D	1	Body	$\frac{3}{4} \times 2\frac{3}{4} \times 2\frac{3}{4}''$
E	1	Boom	$\frac{3}{4} \times 2 \times 18''$
F	1	Crank	$\frac{3}{4} \times 1\frac{1}{4} \times 1\frac{1}{4}''$
G	2	Crank handle	$\frac{1}{4}''$ dowel, $\frac{3}{4}''$ long
H	1	Crankshaft	$\frac{3}{8}''$ dowel, $2\frac{3}{4}''$ long
I	1	Track connector	$\frac{3}{4} \times 2\frac{1}{4} \times 4\frac{3}{8}''$
J	2	Outer track	$\frac{1}{4} \times 1\frac{1}{4} \times 7\frac{1}{2}''$
K	2	Center track	$\frac{3}{4} \times 1\frac{1}{4} \times 7\frac{1}{2}''$
L	2	Inner track	$\frac{1}{4} \times 1\frac{1}{4} \times 7\frac{1}{2}''$
M	1	Body bottom	$\frac{3}{8} \times 3\frac{3}{4} \times 5''$
N	1	Spacer	$1\frac{1}{2} \times 1\frac{1}{2} \times \frac{1}{8}''$
O	1	Pivot post	$\frac{3}{8}''$ dowel, $2\frac{1}{2}''$ long
P	1	Lock washer	$1\frac{1}{4} \times 1\frac{1}{4} \times \frac{3}{8}''$
Q	6	Wheel	$1 \times 1 \times \frac{5}{8}''$
R	6	Axle	$\frac{1}{4}''$ dowel, $1\frac{1}{8}''$ long
S	14	Fake track roller	$\frac{3}{4} \times \frac{3}{4} \times \frac{1}{8}''$
T	1	Take-up wheel	$\frac{5}{8} \times 1\frac{1}{4} \times 1\frac{1}{4}''$

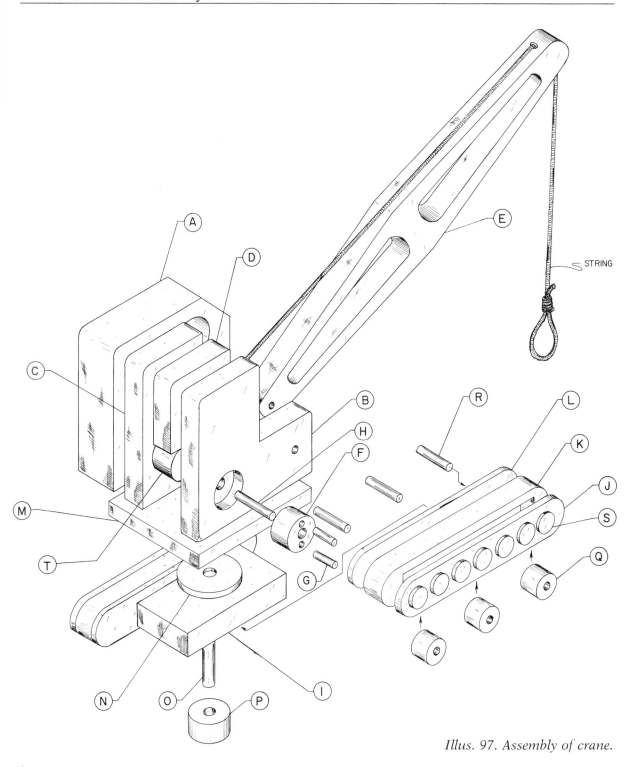

STRING

Illus. 97. Assembly of crane.

TOOLS AND SUPPLIES

Table saw	1¼″ × No. 4 flathead
Drill press	wood screws
Router	Hole saw
Forstner bit	Disc or belt sander
Try square	Twist bit
Nail set	Ruler
Band saw	¼ × 2½″ lag bolt

CONSTRUCTION NOTES

Parts A, B, C, and D (Illus. 98)

Using ¾- or 1½-inch stock, cut out the body parts on a band saw or a jigsaw. Glue parts B, C, and D together to make a unit. Sand the edges of this section. Cut out part A, sand the edges, and then glue part A to parts B, C, and D. Drill the large hole for

NOTE: EACH SQUARE EQUALS 1 INCH

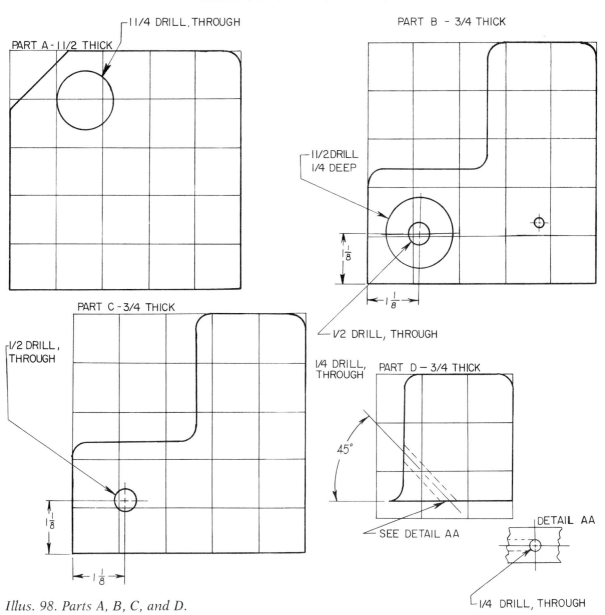

Illus. 98. Parts A, B, C, and D.

the window with a Forstner bit and a drill press. The hole that part F (crank) will fit into can also be drilled with a Forstner bit. (See Illus. 100 for part F.) Twist bits may be used for the other holes. Sand parts A, B, C, and D with a belt sander so that they appear to be one solid piece of wood.

Part E (Illus. 99)

See pages 39–40 for information on how to make part E (boom). Once the center sections are cut out and sanded, drill the holes in the end of the boom with a twist bit and drill press. Slide part E into the body and put the lag bolt in the hole in part B, through the boom, and into parts C and D. Tighten the bolt to make the boom fit firmly and stay in place; remember, however, that the boom should be movable.

Parts F, G, H, and T (Illus. 100)

Parts T (take-up wheel) and F (crank) can both be made with a hole saw and a drill press. Once they have been made, drill the center holes to the required diameters. On part F, drill the hole that part G (crank handle) will fit into. On part T, drill a small hole for the string. The size of this hole will depend on the diameter of the string you buy.

Cut parts G and H (crank shaft) to length. Slide part H through the hole in part B. Glue on part T, then glue part F on the outside. Part F should fit in the hole on part B. This section should turn freely inside the hole in part B.

Glue part G into part F so that the crank handles protrude by approximately ⅜ of an inch. Put the piece of string through the top of part E (boom), and glue it into the small hole in part T. Leave enough string so that part E can be cranked up and down.

Parts J, K, L, Q, R, and S (Illus. 101)

Cut the dowel rod to length for part R (axle). Resaw or plane enough lumber to the correct thickness for parts J (outer track) and L (inner track). Cut parts J, K (center track), and L out with a jigsaw or a band saw. Glue parts L, K, and J together to make one unit. Sand the outside edges so that they look like one smooth board. Drill the holes through part L and into part J.

Cut part Q (wheel) out with a drill press and a hole saw. Put part Q into parts L, J,

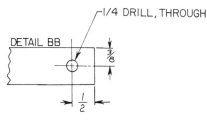

CRANE PARTS

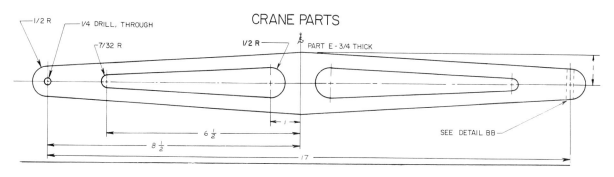

Illus. 99. Part E.

and K, and slide part R through the holes in part L, through part Q, and into part J. Make sure the wheels turn freely and then glue part R into part L.

See pages 39 and 40 for instructions on making part S (fake track roller). Once the fake track rollers are made, space them equally, as shown in Illus. 97, and glue them onto part J.

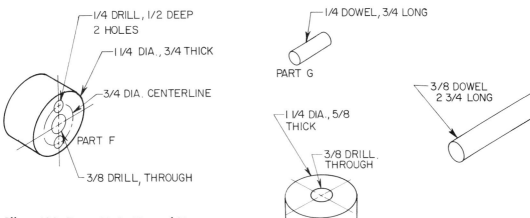

Illus. 100. Parts F, G, H, and T.

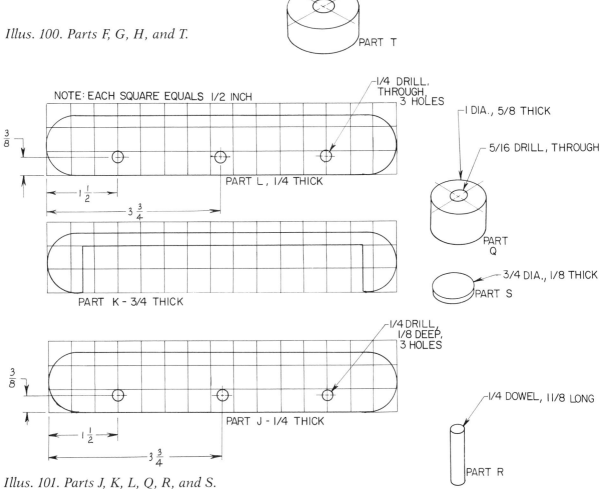

Illus. 101. Parts J, K, L, Q, R, and S.

Part I (Illus. 102)

Part I (track connector) can be cut out with a table saw; the hole can be drilled with a drill press and twist bit. Once Part I is made and sanded, glue parts L, K, and J to part I so that they are flush on top. Part I should be centered from end to end on part L.

Parts M, N, O, and P (Illus. 103 and 104)

Part O (pivot post) should be cut to length. Using a hole saw and a drill press, make parts N (spacer) and P (lock washer). Drill the large holes in parts N and P with a drill press.

Cut part M (body bottom) on the table saw. Using 1¼″ × No. 10 flathead wood screws, attach part M to parts A, B, C, and D (body unit). Glue part O into part M. Place part N onto part O; then put part I (track connector) onto part O, and glue part P onto part O, making sure part I swivels freely.

Illus. 102. Part I.

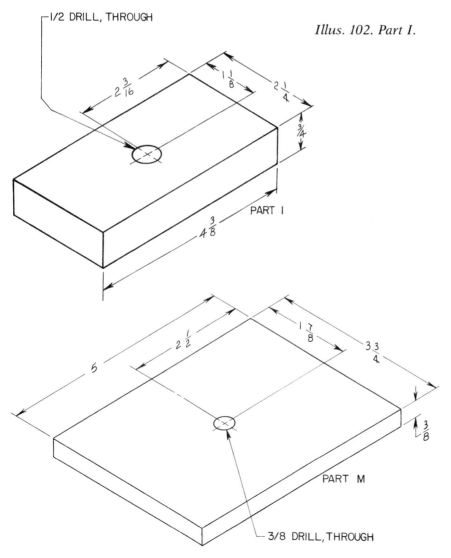

1/2 DRILL, THROUGH

2 3/16   1 1/8   2 1/4

3/4

PART I

4 3/8

Illus. 103. Part M. See Illus. 104 for parts N, O, and P.

5   2 1/2   1 7/8   3 3/4

3/8

PART M

3/8 DRILL, THROUGH

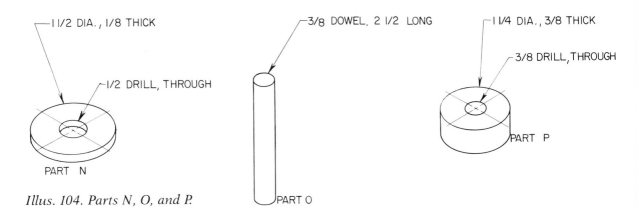

1 1/2 DIA., 1/8 THICK

1/2 DRILL, THROUGH

PART N

3/8 DOWEL, 2 1/2 LONG

PART O

1 1/4 DIA., 3/8 THICK

3/8 DRILL, THROUGH

PART P

Illus. 104. Parts N, O, and P.

Train

Illus. 105. See page A of the color section for a look at the train in full color.

Key to Assembly Shown in Illus. 107

LETTER	NUMBER REQUIRED	PART	SIZE
A	1	Steam engine base	$6^3/8 \times 2^1/4 \times 3/4$" walnut
B	2	Steam engine front axle	$1/4$" dowel, $3^3/8$" long
C	4	Steam engine front wheel	$1^9/16 \times 1^9/16 \times 3/4$" pine or maple
D	2	Steam engine back wheel	$2^3/4 \times 2^3/4 \times 1^1/2$" pine or maple
E	1	Axle support	$3 \times 2^1/4 \times 1/2$" walnut
F	1	Boiler	$1^3/8$" round moulding, 4" long, pine
G	1	Steam dome	$3/4$" dowel, $1^3/4$" long
H	1	Smokestack	$4^1/4 \times 1^1/4 \times 1^1/4$" pine or maple
I	1	Steam engine top	$3^1/2 \times 2^1/4 \times 3/4$" walnut
J	1	Steam engine back axle	$1/4$" dowel, $4^3/4$" long
K	1	Steam engine light	$3/8 \times 3/8 \times 3/8$" walnut
L	1	Passenger car base	$7^1/2 \times 2^1/4 \times 3/4$" walnut
M	8	Passenger and caboose car wheel	$2 \times 2 \times 1^1/8$" pine or maple
N	8	Passenger and caboose car axle	$1/4$" dowel, 4" long
O	1	Passenger car window section	$6^1/4 \times 1^1/2 \times 2$" pine or maple

P	1	Passenger car top	$7\frac{3}{4} \times 2\frac{1}{4} \times \frac{3}{4}$" walnut
Q	1	Caboose base	$5\frac{1}{4} \times 2\frac{1}{4} \times \frac{3}{4}$" walnut
R	1	Caboose window section	$4\frac{5}{8} \times 1\frac{1}{2} \times 3$" pine or maple
S	1	Caboose top, center	$2\frac{3}{4} \times 2\frac{1}{4} \times \frac{3}{4}$" walnut
T	2	Caboose top, end	$1\frac{1}{2} \times 2\frac{1}{4} \times \frac{3}{4}$" walnut
U	1	Steam engine window section	$3\frac{1}{8} \times 2\frac{3}{8} \times 1\frac{1}{2}$" pine or maple

TOOLS AND SUPPLIES

Table saw
Wood lathe
Belt sander
Ruler
Hand-screw or
   C-clamp
Screwdriver
Hand plane
Hole saw
Forstner bit
Glue

Drill press
Coping saw
Radial arm saw
Try square
Electric drill
Wood file
Twist bits
Spade bits
Plug cutter
Band saw

CONSTRUCTION NOTES

Parts A, B, C, D, J, L, M, N, Q
(Illus. 106 and 108)

Start the train by cutting parts A (steam engine base), L (passenger car base), and Q (caboose base) with a table saw, coping saw, or band saw. Cut the three dadoes in part A with the table saw. Use a board that is longer than needed.

Using an electric drill and twist bit, drill the holes in parts L and Q for the axles to fit into. Using a coping saw, cut parts B, J, and

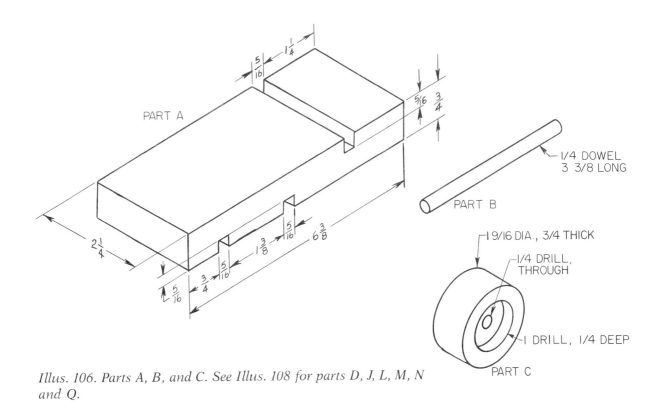

Illus. 106. Parts A, B, and C. See Illus. 108 for parts D, J, L, M, N and Q.

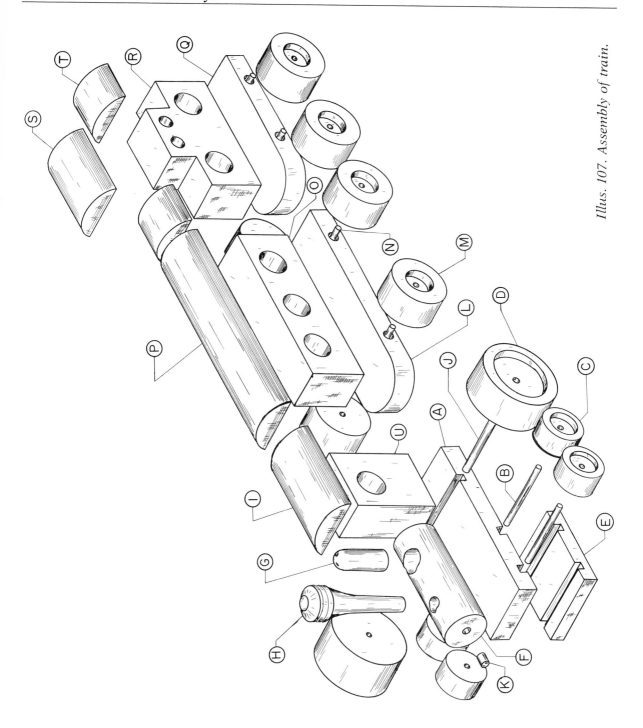

Illus. 107. Assembly of train.

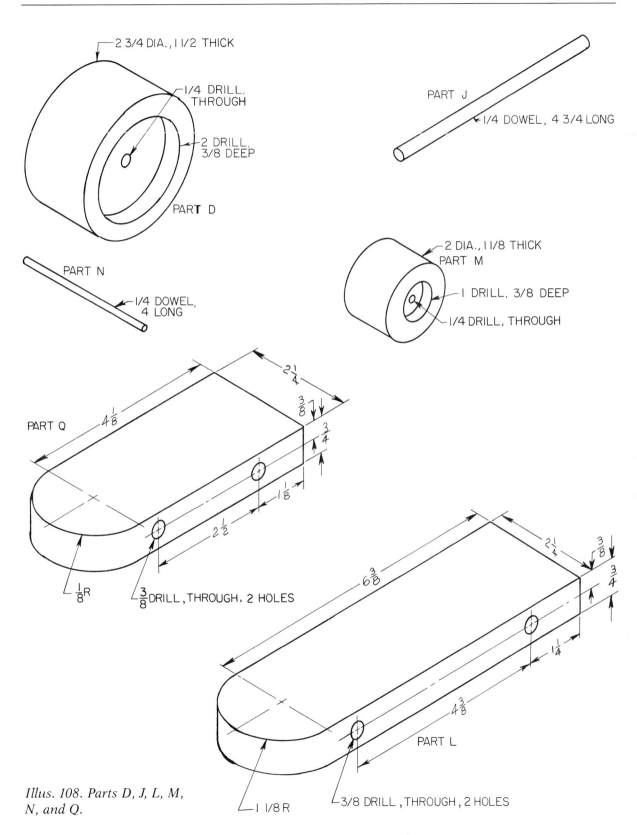

2 3/4 DIA., 1 1/2 THICK

1/4 DRILL, THROUGH

2 DRILL, 3/8 DEEP

PART D

PART J

1/4 DOWEL, 4 3/4 LONG

PART N

1/4 DOWEL, 4 LONG

2 DIA., 1 1/8 THICK
PART M

1 DRILL, 3/8 DEEP

1/4 DRILL, THROUGH

PART Q

$2\frac{1}{4}$

$\frac{3}{8}$

$\frac{3}{4}$

$4\frac{1}{8}$

$1\frac{1}{8}$

$2\frac{1}{2}$

$\frac{1}{8}$R

$\frac{3}{8}$DRILL, THROUGH, 2 HOLES

$2\frac{1}{4}$

$\frac{3}{8}$

$\frac{3}{4}$

$6\frac{3}{8}$

$1\frac{1}{4}$

$4\frac{3}{8}$

PART L

$1\frac{1}{8}$R

3/8 DRILL, THROUGH, 2 HOLES

Illus. 108. Parts D, J, L, M, N, and Q.

N (axles), noting that they are different in length. Using a drill press and a hole saw, make parts C, D, and M (wheels). The recessed portions can be drilled out with a Forstner bit and drill press.

Slide part N through parts L and Q (caboose base). Glue part M onto part N so that the parts are flush on the recessed surface of the wheels. Glue part J into part D, and part B into part C. Parts J and D and B and C should also be flush on the outside recessed part and will be attached to part A later.

Parts, E, F, G, H, and K (Illus. 109)

Cut part E (axle support) with a table saw. Glue and clamp part E to the bottom of part A with part B in the grooves. Cut

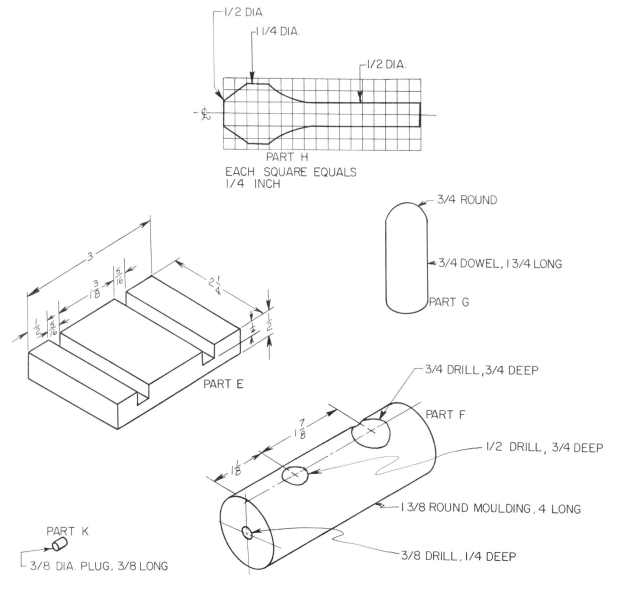

Illus. 109. Parts E, F, G, H, and K.

part F (boiler) to length with a table saw. Drill the three holes with a spade bit and drill press. Attach part F to part A (steam engine base) with two 1¼″ × No. 10 wood screws from the bottom of part A. Parts A and F should be flush on the front, and part F should be centered from side to side on part A.

Cut part G (steam dome) to length with the table saw. Round off the top with a wood file and sand smooth. Glue part G into part F so that part G protrudes out of part F by 1⅛ inch.

Turn part H (smokestack) on a wood lathe. Glue part H into part F, letting it protrude by 3½ inches.

Part K (steam engine light) can be cut with a drill press and a ⅜-inch plug cutter. Glue part K into part F so that part K protrudes out of part F by approximately ³⁄₁₆ of an inch.

Parts, I, O, P, R, S, T, and U (Illus. 110 and 111)

Cut parts R (caboose window section), O (passenger car window section), and U (steam engine window section) with a table

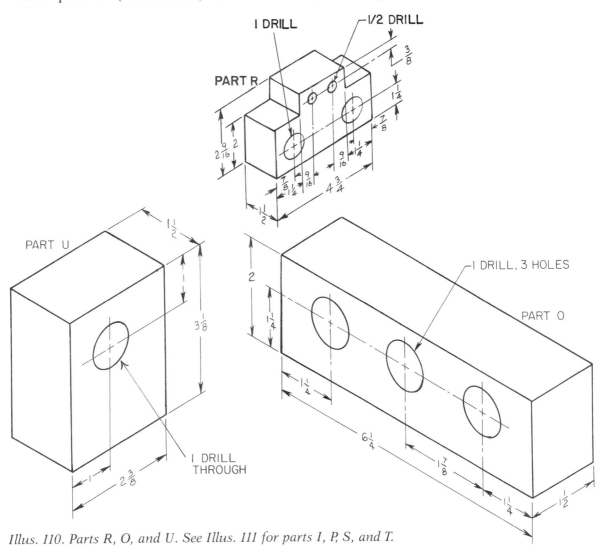

Illus. 110. Parts R, O, and U. See Illus. 111 for parts I, P, S, and T.

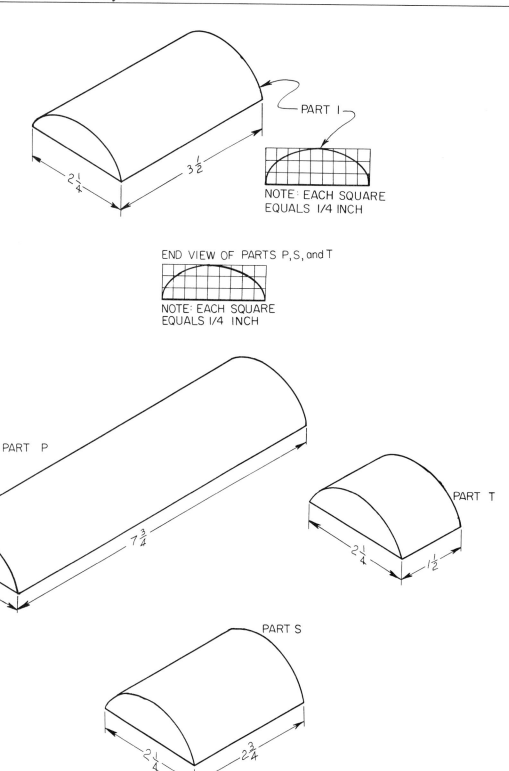

PART I

NOTE: EACH SQUARE
EQUALS 1/4 INCH

END VIEW OF PARTS P, S, and T

NOTE: EACH SQUARE
EQUALS 1/4 INCH

PART P

PART T

PART S

Illus. 111. Parts I, P, S, and T.

saw. Cut the notches in part R with a band saw. Drill the holes in all three parts with a Forstner bit and drill press.

Attach part U to part A with glue and a 1¼″ × No. 10 flathead wood screw from the bottom. Make sure part J is placed in the groove in part A before attaching part U. (See Illus. 108 for part J.) Attach parts O and R in the same manner.

With a table saw, cut a piece of stock long enough to make parts I (steam engine top), P (passenger car top), S (caboose top, center), and T (caboose top, ends). Round these parts by hand with a plane or a rasp. Sand this piece of stock to its round shape with a belt sander. Cut the individual pieces with a radial arm saw. To prevent accidents, hold small parts against the fence on the radial arm saw with scrap board, instead of trying to hold a piece close by hand. Attach these parts to the window sections with glue and 1¼″ × No. 10 flathead wood screws. Plug these screws and sand the tops smooth.

Ironing Board and Iron

IRONING BOARD

Illus. 112.

Key to Assembly Shown in Illus. 113

LETTER	NUMBER REQUIRED	PART	SIZE
A	1	Top	$29 \times 8\frac{1}{4} \times \frac{3}{4}''$
B	4	Leg	$29\frac{1}{4} \times 1\frac{1}{2} \times 1\frac{1}{2}''$
C	2	Brace	$\frac{3}{4} \times 7 \times 1\frac{1}{2}''$

TOOLS AND SUPPLIES

Table saw
Electric hand drill
Dado head
Try square
No. 10 Plug cutter

Jointer
Ruler
Screwdriver
Band saw or jigsaw
Drill press

$1\frac{1}{4}'' \times$ No. 10
    combination drill
    and countersink
$1\frac{1}{4}'' \times$ No. 10 flathead
    wood screws

Illus. 113. Assembly of ironing board.

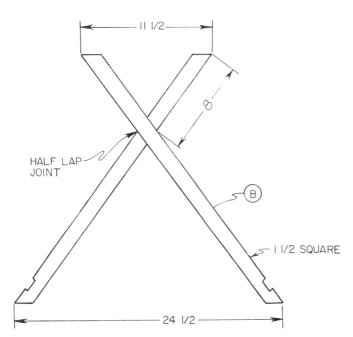

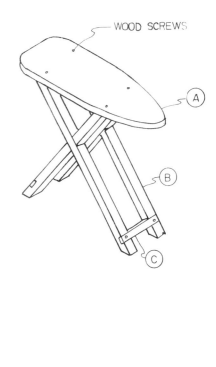

CONSTRUCTION NOTES

Part A (Illus. 114)

Part A (top) can easily be cut out with a band saw or a jigsaw.

Part B (Illus. 115)

Use a jointer to square Part B (legs). The easiest and best method of laying out the half-lap joint is to place the legs on top of each other as shown in Illus. 113. Measure the 24½-inch space at the bottom and the 11½-inch space at the top. Then mark the half-lap, using the legs to mark each other. Cut the required angle on a table saw, using a dado head. Also cut the notch that part C (brace) will fit into. Cut the angles at the top and the bottom of part B with a table saw.

Part C (Illus. 116)

Cut part C (brace) with a table saw. Fit the two legs together. They should fit firmly and require only glue. Place part C into the dado cut on part B. Keep the outsides of parts B and C flush. Using a 1¼″ × No. 10 combination drill and countersink, drill a hole through the brace and into the leg. Screw these parts together with a 1¼″ × No. 10 flathead wood screw and cover the screw with a wood plug. These plugs can be made with a No. 10 plug cutter on a drill press.

Place part A (top) on the legs so that the legs are approximately centered. Make sure the legs are the same distance apart; this distance should be the length of part C at the top and at the bottom of the legs. Attach part A to the legs with 1¼″ × No. 10 flathead wood screws. Cover the screws with plugs and sand smoothly.

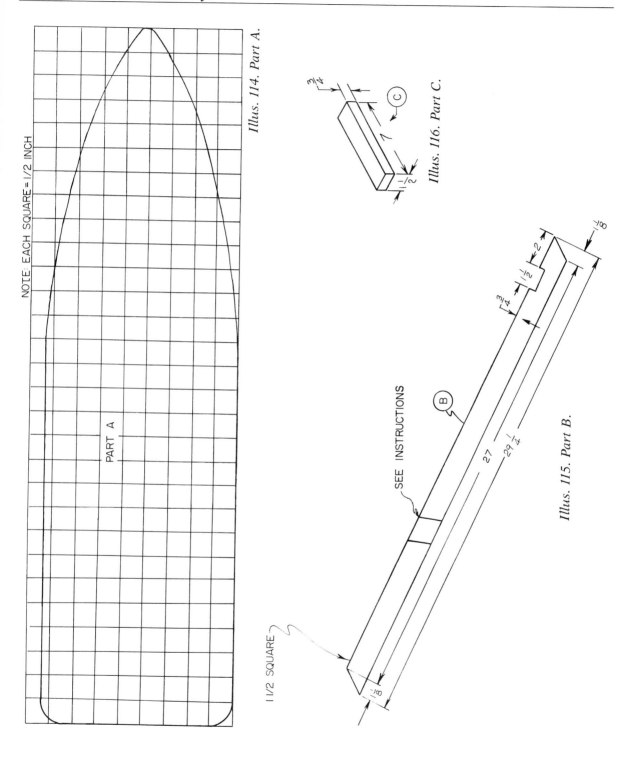

NOTE: EACH SQUARE = 1/2 INCH

PART A

Illus. 114. Part A.

Illus. 116. Part C.

SEE INSTRUCTIONS

Illus. 115. Part B.

1 1/2 SQUARE

IRON

Illus. 117.

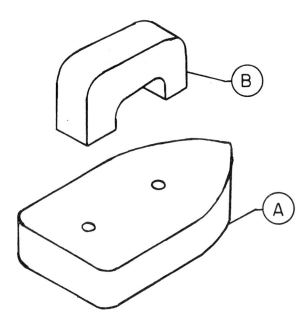

Illus. 118. Assembly of iron. See page F of the color section for a look at the iron in full color.

Key to Assembly Shown in Illus. 118.

LETTER	NUMBER REQUIRED	PART	SIZE
A	1	Base	$7^{1}/_{8} \times 4 \times 1^{1}/_{4}$"
B	1	Handle	$4^{3}/_{4} \times 2^{1}/_{2} \times 1^{1}/_{4}$"

TOOLS AND SUPPLIES

Band saw
Screwdriver
$1^{1}/_{4}$" × No. 10 combination drill and countersink
$1^{1}/_{4}$" × No. 10 flathead wood screws

Try square
Ruler
Jointer
Electric hand drill

CONSTRUCTION NOTES

Parts A and B (Illus. 119)

Plane enough stock with a jointer to make parts A (base) and B (handle). Cut parts A and B out with a band saw. Attach part B to part A with wood screws from the bottom of part A. Use an electric hand drill and a combination wood drill and countersink to predrill the holes for the screws. Sand and finish the project as you desire.

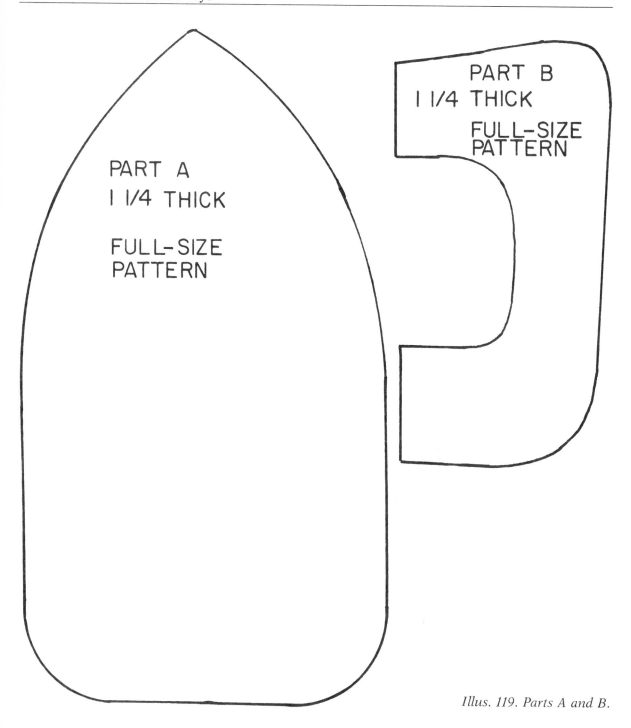

PART A
1 1/4 THICK

FULL-SIZE
PATTERN

PART B
1 1/4 THICK

FULL-SIZE
PATTERN

Illus. 119. Parts A and B.

Toaster

Illus. 120. See page F of the color section for a look at the toaster in full color.

Key to Assembly Shown in Illus. 121

LETTER	NUMBER REQUIRED	PART	SIZE
A	2	Side	$7^{1}/_2 \times 4^{1}/_2 \times {}^{3}/_4''$
B	4	Top spacer	$1^{3}/_4 \times 2^{3}/_4 \times {}^{7}/_{16}''$
C	2	Center	$7^{1}/_2 \times 4^{1}/_2 \times {}^{3}/_4''$
D	4	Bottom spacer	$1 \times {}^{3}/_4 \times {}^{7}/_{16}''$
E	2	Pivot dowel	$^{1}/_8''$ dowel, 2" long
F	1	Bottom	$7^{1}/_2 \times 4^{1}/_2 \times {}^{3}/_4''$
G	2	Toast lifter	$6^{1}/_2 \times {}^{1}/_2 \times {}^{1}/_4''$
H	3	Dowel	$^{1}/_4''$ dowel, $2^{3}/_8''$ long
I	2	Toast	$3^{3}/_4 \times 3^{1}/_2 \times {}^{3}/_8''$

TOOLS AND SUPPLIES

Jointer
Table saw
Twist bit
Ruler

Planer
Belt sander
Try square
Screwdriver

Band saw
$1^{1}/_4'' \times$ No. 10 combination drill and countersink

$1^{1}/_4'' \times$ No. 10 flathead wood screws
Hammer

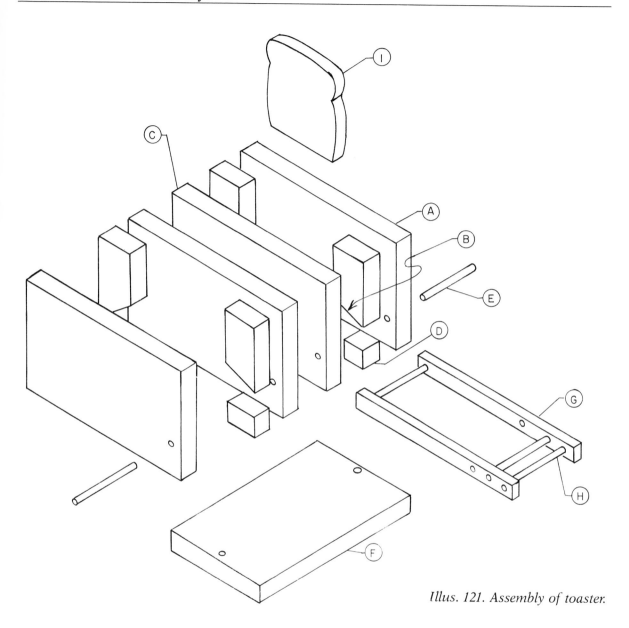

Illus. 121. Assembly of toaster.

CONSTRUCTION NOTES

All of the parts on the toaster are made of cherry except part I (toast) and parts E and H (dowel rods). The toast is made from mahogany. The dowels are made of birch.

Parts A, B, C, and D (Illus. 122)

Plane parts A (side), B (top spacer), C (center), and D (bottom spacer) to their correct thicknesses. Use a table saw to cut these pieces to their correct sizes. A band saw can be used to cut the angle on part B.

Glue these parts together as shown in Illus. 121, and drill the hole that part E (pivot dowel) will fit into. (See Illus. 123 for part E.) Once these parts are one unit, round the top and side edges as shown in Illus. 120. They can be rounded with a band saw and then sanded smooth with a belt sander.

Parts E, G, and H (Illus. 123)

Cut part G (toast lifter) with the table saw; drill the holes with a drill press and twist bit. Cut part H (dowel), and glue only the two outside dowels for part H into part G. Parts G and H should be flush on the outside.

Slide part G into the end of the toaster,

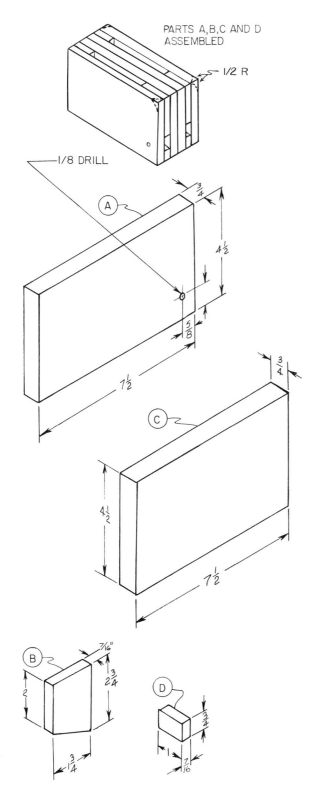

Illus. 122. Parts A, B, C, and D.

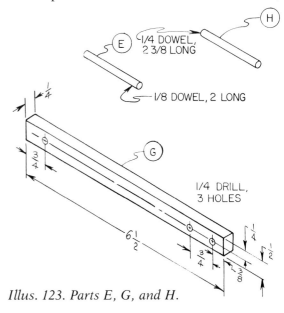

Illus. 123. Parts E, G, and H.

letting it protrude out of the bottom. Glue the remaining dowel for part H into part G, again making sure parts G and H are flush on the outside. Cut part E and slide it into parts A and C, making sure it goes through part G. Part G should swivel easily on part E. When part G on the outside of the toaster is pushed down, part G on the inside should be going up, thus lifting the toast.

Parts F and I (Illus. 124)

Cut part F (bottom) with a table saw and screw it to the bottom of the toaster unit. Sand the corners and edges so that they match the toaster unit. Do not glue part F on; this way, the toaster can be easily taken apart if parts E, G, and H have to be repaired. Part I (toast) is made from mahogany and can be cut out with a band saw.

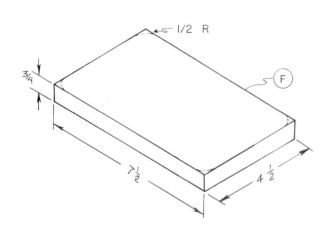

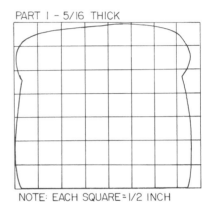

Illus. 124. Parts F and I.

Vacuum Cleaner

Illus. 125.

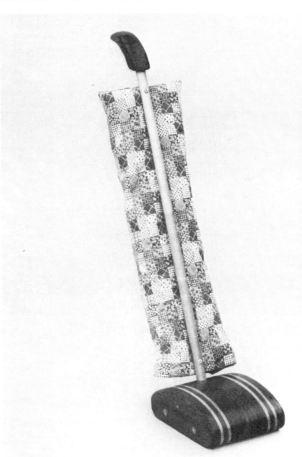

Key to Assembly Shown in Illus. 126

LETTER	NUMBER REQUIRED	PART	SIZE
A	6	Frame	$3 \times 9 \times \frac{3}{4}''$
B	4	Frame	$3 \times 9 \ \frac{1}{4}''$
C	4	Wheel	$2 \times 2 \times \frac{9}{16}''$
D	4	Axle	$\frac{1}{2}''$ dowel, 2" long
E	1	Shaft	$\frac{3}{4}''$ dowel, 26" long
F	1	Handle	$5\frac{1}{2} \times 2\frac{1}{2} \times 1\frac{3}{8}''$
G	2	Inner frame	$3 \times 9 \times \frac{1}{2}''$

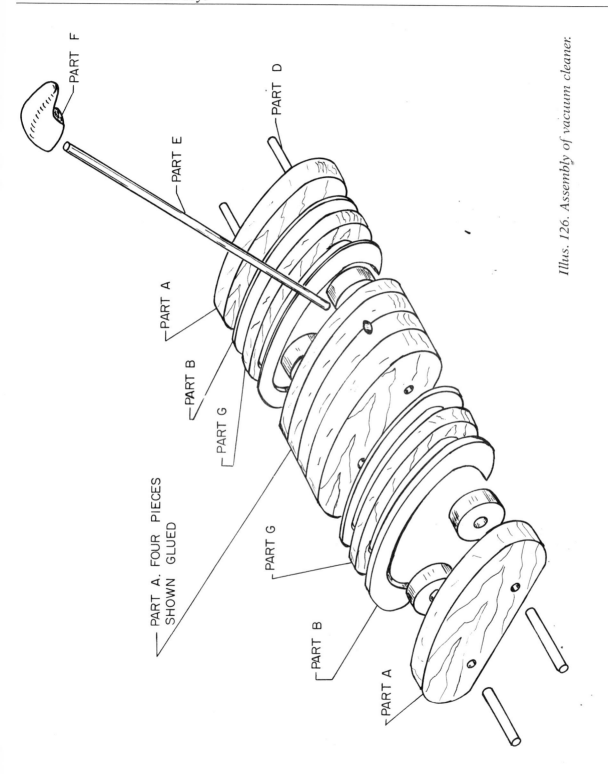

PART F

PART E

PART D

PART A

PART B

PART G

PART A. FOUR PIECES
SHOWN GLUED

PART G

PART B

PART A

Illus. 126. Assembly of vacuum cleaner.

TOOLS AND SUPPLIES

Table saw	*Band saw*
Drill press	*Jointer*
Try square	*Ruler*
Hammer	*Hole saw*
Twist bits	*Belt sander*
File	*Spade bit*
Forstner bit	*Hand-screw clamp*
Glue	

CONSTRUCTION NOTES

Parts A, B, and G (Illus. 126)

Plane stock to the correct thickness for parts A, B, and G (frames). Parts A and G are made of walnut. Part B is made of maple. Cut these parts out with a band saw.

Glue them together and sand their shapes smooth with a belt sander so that they appear to be one part. Using a drill press, drill the holes in part A to receive parts D (axle) and E (shaft). (See Illus. 128 for part D and Illus. 129 for part E.)

Parts C and D (Illus. 128)

Using a hole saw and drill press, make part C (wheel). Drill out the hole in part C with a twist bit, and cut out part D (axle). Slide part D through the hole in part A, through the wheel, and glue it into the center section of part A. Make sure that the wheels do not get glue on them and that they turn freely. Using a belt sander, sand the outsides of parts A and D flush.

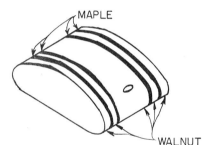

MAPLE

WALNUT

NOTE: EACH SQUARE = 1/2 INCH

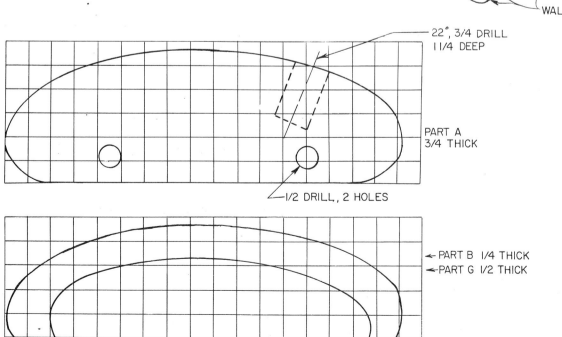

22°, 3/4 DRILL
1 1/4 DEEP

PART A
3/4 THICK

1/2 DRILL, 2 HOLES

◄ PART B 1/4 THICK
◄ PART G 1/2 THICK

Illus. 127. Parts A, B, and G.

Parts E and F (Illus. 129)

Cut a dowel rod to the correct length for part E (shaft). Part F (handle) should be cut out with a band saw. Part F is made of walnut. Use a hand-screw clamp to hold the handle while it is being drilled on the drill press with a spade or Forstner bit. Glue part E into part A and part E into part F. Make sure part F is aligned straight or parallel with the vacuum cleaner.

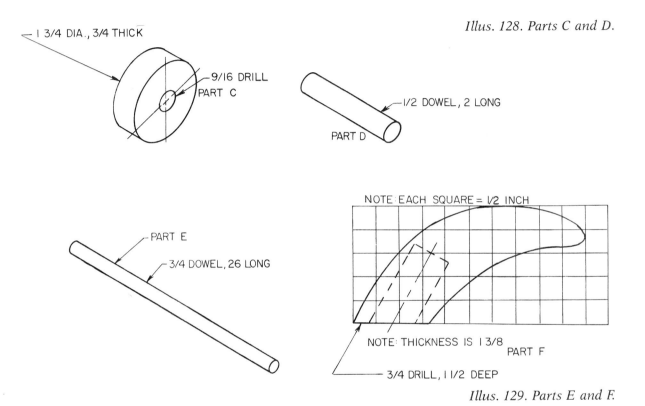

Illus. 128. Parts C and D.

Illus. 129. Parts E and F.

Stove

Illus. 130.

Key to Assembly Shown in Illus. 131

LETTER	NUMBER REQUIRED	PART	SIZE
A	2	Side	$22^{1}/_{4} \times 11^{1}/_{2} \times ^{3}/_{4}"$ birch plywood
B	1	Back	$22 \times 22 \times ^{1}/_{4}"$ plywood
C	1	Shelf	$22 \times 11^{1}/_{4} \times ^{3}/_{4}"$ birch plywood
D	1	Lower horizontal facing	$19^{3}/_{4} \times 6 \times ^{3}/_{4}"$ birch
E	1	Upper horizontal facing	$19^{3}/_{4} \times 4^{1}/_{2} \times ^{3}/_{4}"$ birch
F	2	Vertical facing	$22^{1}/_{4} \times 1^{1}/_{2} \times ^{3}/_{4}"$ birch
G	4	Knob	$1^{3}/_{4} \times 1^{3}/_{4} \times ^{3}/_{4}"$ walnut
H	4	Knob handle	$1^{3}/_{4} \times ^{1}/_{4} \times ^{3}/_{4}"$ maple
I	4	Knob shaft	$^{1}/_{4}"$ dowel, 2" long
J	4	Knob lock	$1^{3}/_{4} \times 1^{3}/_{4} \times ^{3}/_{4}"$ pine
K	1	Door	$20^{1}/_{2} \times 12^{1}/_{2} \times ^{3}/_{4}"$ birch plywood
L	1	Door handle	$8^{1}/_{4} \times ^{5}/_{8} \times 1"$ walnut
M	4	Shelf adjustment bracket	$16^{1}/_{4} \times 1^{1}/_{2} \times ^{3}/_{4}"$ plywood

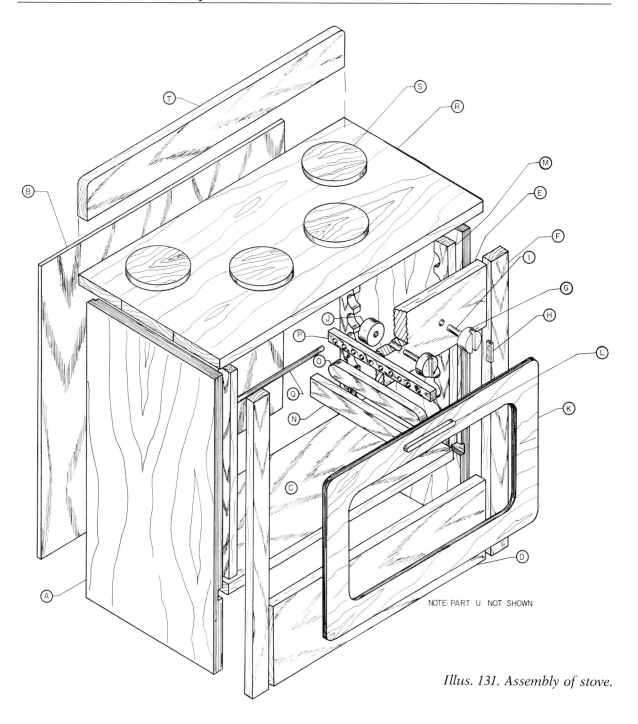

Illus. 131. Assembly of stove.

NOTE: PART U NOT SHOWN

N	4	Shelf support	$10^{1}/_{2} \times 1^{1}/_{4} \times {}^{3}/_{4}''$ pine
O	4	Bracket insert	$10^{1}/_{4} \times 1^{1}/_{4} \times {}^{3}/_{4}''$ pine
P	4	Shelf side	$11 \times {}^{3}/_{4} \times {}^{3}/_{4}''$ pine
Q	20	Shelf rod	${}^{3}/_{8}''$ dowel, 19" long
R	1	Top	$23^{3}/_{4} \times 12^{3}/_{4} \times {}^{3}/_{4}''$ birch
S	1	Eye	$5^{1}/_{2} \times 5^{1}/_{2} \times {}^{1}/_{4}''$ walnut
T	1	Top back	$23^{3}/_{4} \times 3 \times {}^{3}/_{4}''$ birch
U	1	Plexiglas™ window	$17 \times 9 \times {}^{3}/_{32}''$ approximately

TOOLS AND SUPPLIES

Radial arm saw
Table saw
Nail set
Jointer
Dado head
Drill press
Band saw
Jigsaw or sabre saw
Router
Ruler
Try square
Glue
Belt sander
Hammer
${}^{3}/_{8}''$ drill bit

Hole saw
Screwdriver
No. 10 plug cutter
Straight-cutting
   router bit
${}^{5}/_{8}''$ sheet-metal screws
No. 6 finishing nails
No. 4 ring-shank
   nails
$1^{1}/_{4}'' \times$ No. 10 flathead
   wood screws
$1^{1}/_{4}'' \times$ No. 10
   combination drill
   and countersink

CONSTRUCTION NOTES

The stove, sink (page 127), and refrigerator (page 134) are all made with construction techniques similar to those used when building quality kitchen cabinets. These toys are built to take rough treatment from children, and should last for several generations.

Parts A, B, and C (Illus. 132)

Cut parts A (side) and C (shelf) out with a table saw. The rabbet joint can be cut with a jointer or table saw, as described on pages 40 and 41. The dado joint can easily be cut on the table saw or radial arm saw or with a router. Part B (back) can also be cut on the table saw.

Once parts A, B, and C are cut, assemble them with glue and a couple of No. 6 finishing nails driven from part A into part C. The back can be attached with No. 4 ring-shank nails.

Parts M, N, O, P, and Q (Illus. 133)

Page 42 describes how to make part M (shelf adjustment bracket). Once part M has been made, mount the shelf adjustment brackets into the stove with $1^{1}/_{4}'' \times$ No. 10 flathead wood screws. Cut parts N (shelf support) and O (bracket insert) and attach them together with glue so that they are flush on top. Part P (shelf side) should be cut; the shelf sides should then be drilled together to ensure straight alignment of part Q (shelf rod). Once parts P and Q are made, glue them together so that they are flush on the outside of part P.

Parts N and O should rest in the round section of part M. Part N should protrude enough to allow the shelf to rest upon parts N and O. This method of adjusting shelves is occasionally found in antique furniture.

Parts D, E, and F (Illus. 134)

Parts D, E, and F (facing) can be cut with either the table saw or the radial arm saw. If possible, use the table saw for ripping opera-

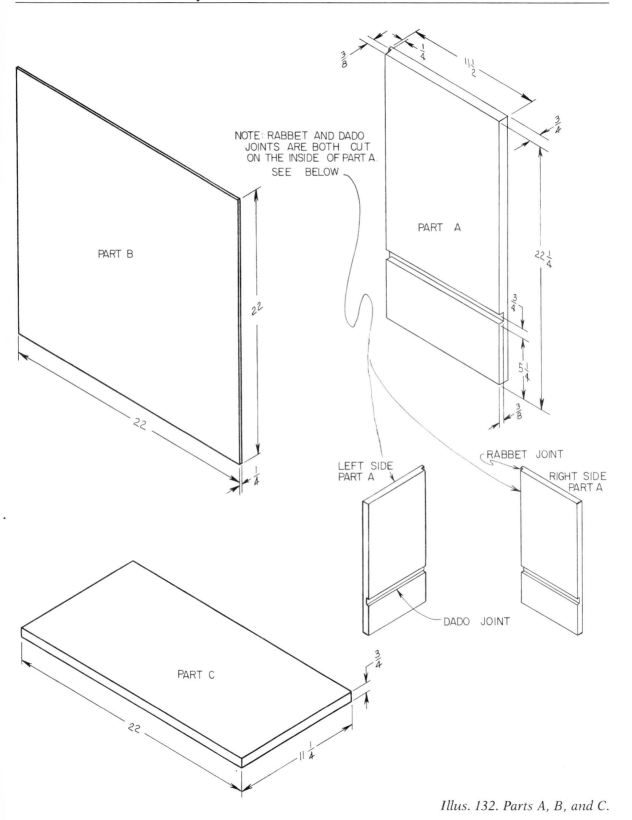

NOTE: RABBET AND DADO
JOINTS ARE BOTH CUT
ON THE INSIDE OF PART A.
SEE BELOW

PART B

PART A

PART C

LEFT SIDE
PART A

RABBET JOINT

RIGHT SIDE
PART A

DADO JOINT

Illus. 132. Parts A, B, and C.

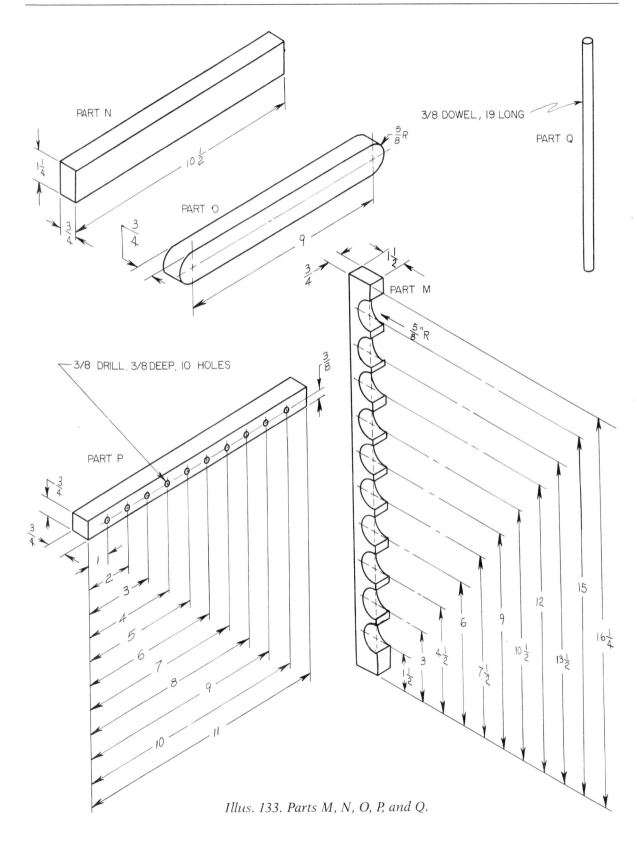

Illus. 133. Parts M, N, O, P, and Q.

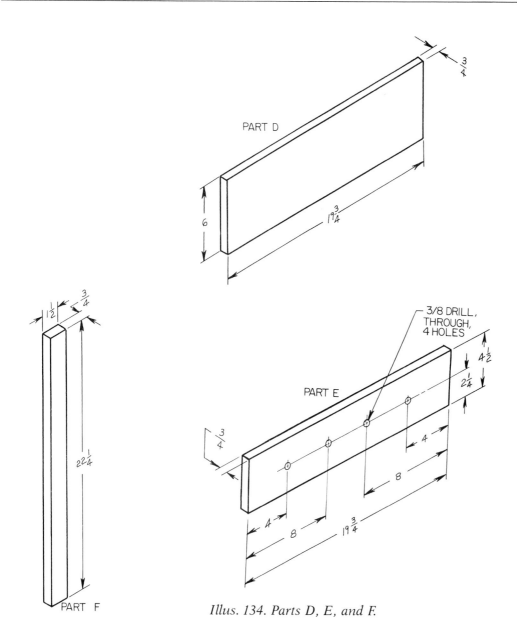

Illus. 134. Parts D, E, and F.

tions because the table saw can perform them more safely than the radial arm saw. Drill the holes in part E (upper horizontal face) into which will later be fitted part I (knob shaft). (See Illus. 135 for part I.)

Part F (vertical facing) should be attached to the stove so that it is flush on the outside with part A (side). Use 1¼″ × No. 10 flathead wood screws and predrill the holes using a 1¼″ × No. 10 combination drill and countersink. Use a No. 10 plug cutter to make plugs to cover the screws. Glue the plugs in and sand the front of part F smooth. Part E can be attached to part M with 1¼″ × No. 10 wood screws. Part D (lower horizontal facing) can be attached to part C (shelf) with the use of wood screws.

Parts G, H, I, and J (Illus. 135)

Pages 42 and 43 describe how to make part G (knob). Once the four knobs are made, glue part H (knob handle) into part G. Next, glue part I (knob shaft) into parts G and J (knob lock). The appliance knob should turn freely in the hole in part E (upper horizontal facing).

Parts K, L, and U (Illus. 136)

Part K (door) can be cut out with the table saw; the corners can be rounded with a band saw or jigsaw. The inside portion of part K can be cut out with a jigsaw or a hand-held sabre saw. Rout out the rabbet that part U (Plexiglas™ window) will fit into; use a straight-cutting router bit for the cut. Attach the Plexiglas™ window with sheet-metal screws.

Part L (door handle) can be cut on a band saw or a jigsaw. Attach it to part K, using 1¼″ × No. 10 wood screws from the back side of part K. Part K can be attached to part D with ordinary offset kitchen cabinet hinges. A magnetic catch can be used at the top to hold the door shut. You may want to attach a string or a chain to the door and to part F to hold the door when it is opened.

Parts R, S, and T (Illus. 137)

Plane or resaw a board for the correct thickness for part S (eye). Cut the round shape out with a band saw or jigsaw. Glue enough stock for part R (top), and cut it to size on a table saw. Cut part T (top back) and attach it to part R with wood screws from the bottom of part R. Glue part S to part R, as shown in Illus. 137. Once these parts have been assembled, drill holes into the top of part R using a 1¼″ × No. 10 combination drill and attach part R to part A with wood screws. Fill these holes with wooden plugs and sand smoothly.

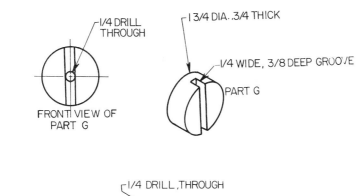
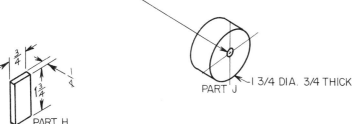
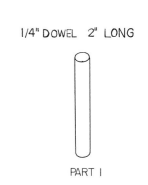

Illus. 135. Parts G, H, I, and J.

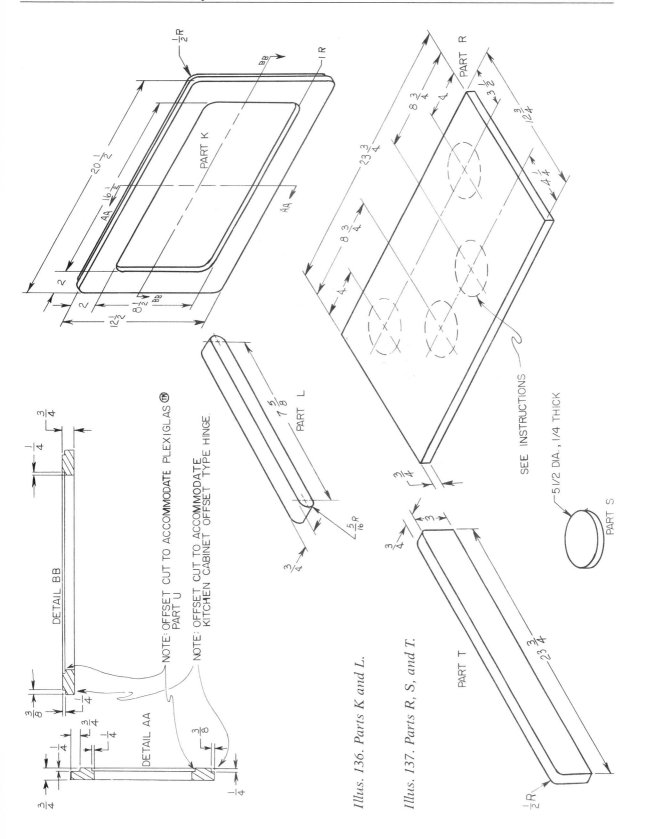

Illus. 136. Parts K and L.

Illus. 137. Parts R, S, and T.

Sink

Illus. 138.

Key to Assembly Shown in Illus. 139

LETTER	NUMBER REQUIRED	PART	SIZE
A	2	Side	$22^{1}/_{4} \times 11^{1}/_{2} \times {}^{3}/_{4}$" birch
B	1	Back	$22 \times 22 \times {}^{1}/_{4}$"
C	1	Bottom shelf	$11^{1}/_{4} \times 22 \times {}^{3}/_{4}$"
D	3	Horizontal facing	$19 \times 2 \times {}^{3}/_{4}$" birch
E	2	Vertical facing	$22^{1}/_{4} \times 2 \times {}^{3}/_{4}$"
F	1	Vertical facing	$2^{1}/_{4} \times 2 \times {}^{3}/_{4}$"
G	1	Vertical facing	$14 \times 2 \times {}^{3}/_{4}$"
H	2	Door	$14^{3}/_{8} \times 9 \times {}^{3}/_{4}$" birch
I	1	Brace	$22 \times 2 \times {}^{3}/_{4}$"

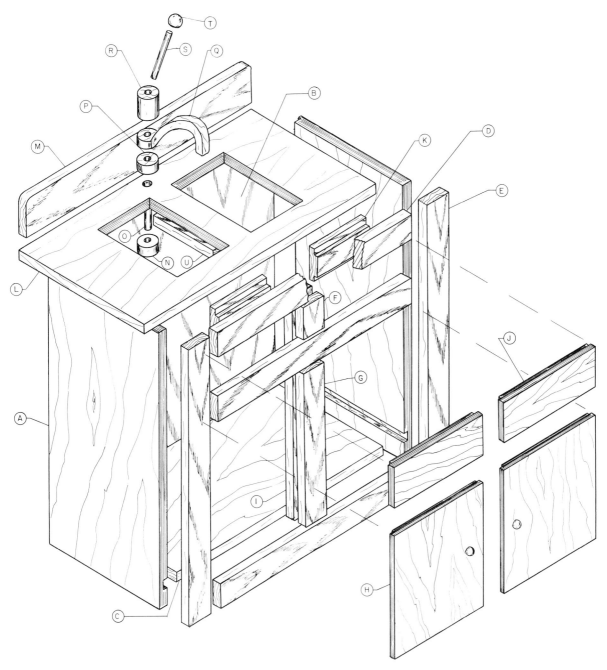

Illus. 139. Assembly of sink.

J	2	Fake drawer front	$3 \times 9 \times \frac{3}{4}''$ birch
K	2	Drawer support	$3 \times 7 \times \frac{3}{4}''$
L	1	Top	$24 \times 12\frac{3}{4} \times \frac{3}{4}''$ cherry or mahogany
M	1	Top back	$24 \times 3 \times \frac{3}{4}''$ cherry or mahogany
N	1	Locking washer	$1\frac{3}{4} \times 1\frac{3}{4} \times \frac{3}{4}''$
O	1	Faucet shaft	$\frac{1}{2}''$ dowel, $4\frac{1}{2}''$ long
P	1	Spacing washer	$1\frac{3}{4} \times 1\frac{3}{4} \times \frac{3}{4}''$
Q	1	Faucet	$11 \times 4 \times 2''$
R	1	Faucet top	$1\frac{3}{4} \times 1\frac{3}{4} \times 1\frac{1}{2}''$
S	1	Faucet handle	$\frac{1}{2}''$ dowel, $3\frac{1}{2}''$ long
T	1	Faucet knob	$1''$ round knob
U	1	Brace	$2 \times 8 \times \frac{3}{4}''$
V	2	Bowl	Approximate size $5\frac{1}{4} \times 8''$ plastic

TOOLS AND SUPPLIES

Radial arm saw — Hole saw
Table saw — Screwdriver
Jointer — No. 10 plug cutter
Dado head — Straight-cutting
Drill press — router bit
Band saw — $\frac{5}{8}''$ sheet-metal screws
Jigsaw or sabre saw — No. 6 finishing nails
Router — No. 4 ring-shank
Ruler — nails
Try square — $1\frac{1}{4}'' \times$ No. 10 flathead
Glue — screws
Hammer — $1\frac{1}{4}'' \times$ No. 10
Nail set — combination drill
$\frac{3}{8}''$ drill bit — bit

CONSTRUCTION NOTES

Parts A, B, and C (Illus. 140 and 141)

Cut part A (side) out with a table saw. The rabbet and dado joints can also be cut with a table saw.

Cut parts B (back) and part C (bottom shelf) to size with the table saw. Glue part C into part A and nail in a couple of No. 6 finishing nails. Part B should fit into the rabbet joint on part A. Nail part B to part A and to part C with No. 4 ring-shank nails.

NOTE: THE TWO PIECES USED FOR PART A ARE CUT ON OPPOSITE SIDES.

LEFT SIDE PART A

RIGHT SIDE PART A

Illus. 140. Part A. See Illus. 141 for parts B and C.

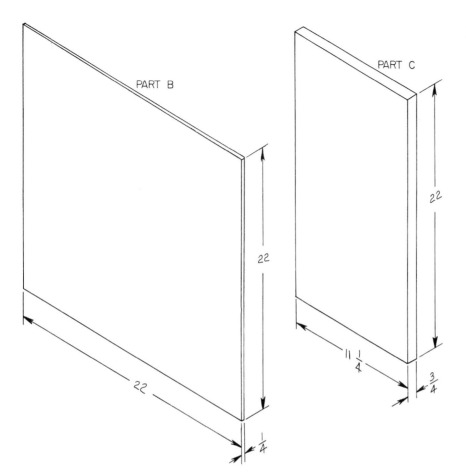

Illus. 141. Parts B and C.

PART B

PART C

22

22

22

11 1/4

3/4

1/4

Parts D, E, F, G, and I
(Illus. 142 and 143)

Cut part E (vertical facing) on the table saw first. Attach part E to part A with 1¼″ × No. 10 flathead wood screws. Cover the screws with wood plugs made with a No. 10 plug cutter.

Next, cut part D (horizontal facing). The center and top pieces used for part D will require a small block of wood that is screwed behind them and also screwed into part E. The bottom board used for part D can be attached to part C (bottom shelf) with wood screws covered with plugs. Part I (brace) is attached from the back side to part D.

Next, cut parts F (small vertical brace) and G (vertical facing) to fit these individ-

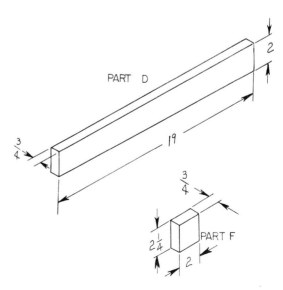

PART D

2

3/4

19

3/4

2 1/4

PART F

2

Illus. 142. Parts D and F. See Illus. 143 for parts E, G, and I.

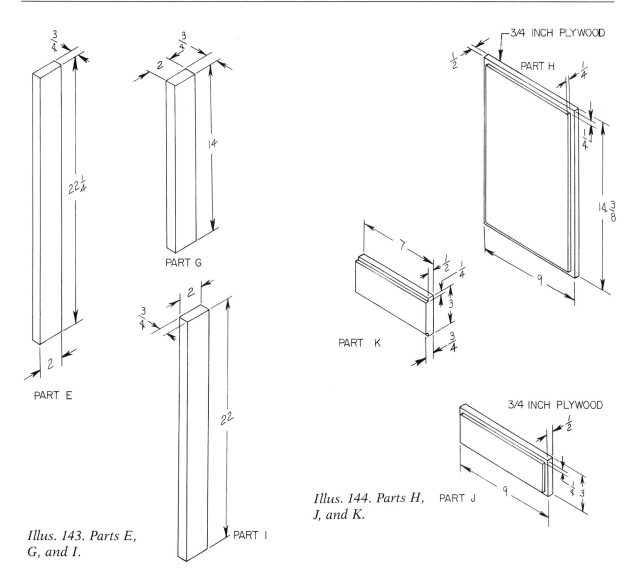

Illus. 143. Parts E, G, and I.

Illus. 144. Parts H, J, and K.

ual spaces. Attach parts F and G to part I by drilling from the back of part I and using 1¼″ × No. 10 flathead screws; plugging is not necessary.

Parts H, J, and K (Illus. 144)

Parts H (doors) and J (fake drawer front) can be cut out with the table saw. The rabbet joint can be cut with either a jointer or a table saw; see pages 40 and 41 for instructions.

Cut part K (drawer support) in one long section. Cut the rabbet joints while the piece of stock is still in a long section; then cut both pieces to their required length. This method is safer than cutting two smaller pieces.

Place part K inside the sink and, with 1¼″ × No. 10 flathead wood screws, attach it to part J (fake drawer front). Part H should be mounted on the sink with regular offset spring-loaded kitchen cabinet hinges.

Once the doors are in place and work properly, drill the holes for the doorknobs you have selected and attach the knobs to the doors.

Parts L, M, U, and V (Illus. 145)

Parts L (top) and M (top back) should be made from solid wood. Cut the parts out with a table saw; then use a jigsaw or sabre saw to cut the holes out for part V (plastic bowls you have selected). Round the corners on part M with a jigsaw. Attach part M to part L with 1¼″ × No. 10 flathead wood screws that are attached from the bottom of part L into the bottom of part M. Parts M and L should be flush on the back.

Part U is a brace used to strengthen part L. Since wood breaks easily across the grain, the center of part L is a weak point in the design. Make sure the grain in part U runs with the length of the board.

Parts N, O, P, Q, R, S, and T (Illus. 146)

Parts N (locking washer), P (spacing washer), and R (faucet top) can be made on a drill press using a hole saw. Drill the centers out to the required hole sizes. Cut parts O (faucet shaft) and S (faucet handle) to their required lengths.

Part T is a doorknob made of maple that can be found in most hardware or lumber stores. This part could also be easily turned on a wood lathe. Glue part T onto part S; then glue part S into the slanted hole in part R. When making part Q (faucet), cut the shape out with a band saw. Assemble parts N, O, P, Q, and R with glue, as shown in Illus. 139. Be sure to allow clearance for these parts so that they can turn freely.

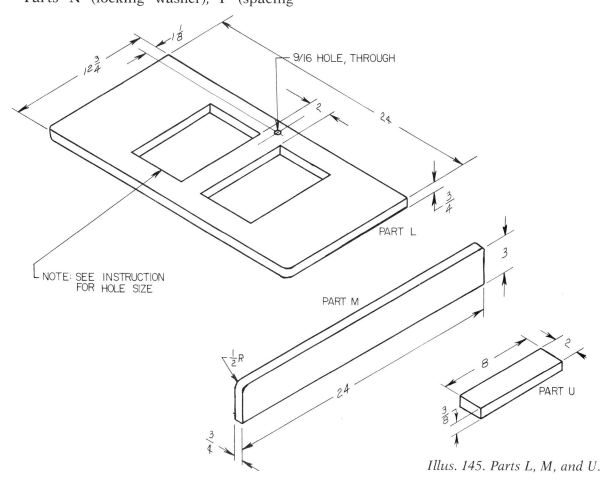

Illus. 145. Parts L, M, and U.

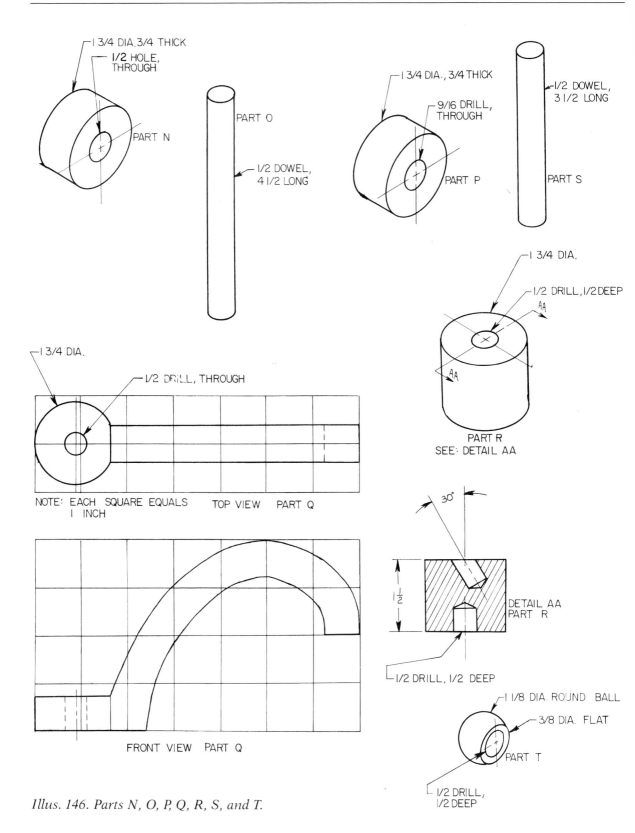

Illus. 146. Parts N, O, P, Q, R, S, and T.

Refrigerator and Freezer

Illus. 147.

Key to Assembly Shown in Illus. 148

LETTER	NUMBER REQUIRED	PART	SIZE
A	2	Side	$11^{1}/_{2} \times {}^{3}/_{4} \times 36''$
B	1	Back	$24 \times 36 \times {}^{1}/_{4}''$
C	1	Bottom	$24 \times 11^{1}/_{4} \times {}^{3}/_{4}''$
D	1	Top	$24^{3}/_{4} \times 12^{1}/_{4} \times {}^{3}/_{4}''$

E	2	Vertical facing	$24^3/_4 \times 1^1/_2 \times {}^3/_4''$
F	3	Horizontal facing	$33 \times 1^1/_2 \times {}^3/_4''$
G	1	Center board	$35^5/_8 \times 11^1/_4 \times {}^3/_4''$
H	1	Refrigerator door front	$35^3/_4 \times 15^1/_2 \times {}^3/_4''$
I	1	Freezer door front	$35^3/_4 \times 8^1/_2 \times {}^3/_4''$
J	2	Freezer door horizontal moulding	$8^1/_2 \times 1^1/_2 \times {}^3/_4''$
K	4	Freezer and refrigerator vertical moulding	$34 \times 1^1/_2 \times {}^3/_4''$
L	2	Refrigerator door horizontal moulding	$15^1/_2 \times 1^1/_2 \times {}^3/_4''$
M	2	Handle	$9^1/_2 \times {}^3/_4 \times {}^3/_4''$
N	2	Front and back base	$24^3/_4 \times {}^3/_4 \times {}^3/_4''$
O	2	Side base	$10^3/_4 \times {}^3/_4 \times {}^3/_4''$
P	8	Shelf adjustment bracket	$1 \times {}^3/_4 \times 32^1/_2''$
Q	16	Shelf support	${}^3/_4 \times 1^1/_4 \times 10^1/_2''$
R	16	Bracket insert	${}^3/_4 \times 1^1/_2 \times 10^1/_2''$
S	16	Shelf side	${}^3/_4 \times {}^3/_4 \times 11''$
T	40	Refrigerator shelf rod	${}^3/_8''$ dowel, $12^1/_2''$ long
U	40	Freezer shelf rod	${}^3/_8''$ dowel, $5^3/_8''$ long

TOOLS AND SUPPLIES

Table saw
Jointer
Drill press
Try square
Nail set
$1^1/_4'' \times$ No. 10 flathead wood screws
No. 4 ring-shank nails
Twist bit
Glue

$1^1/_4'' \times$ No. 10 combination drill
Screwdriver
No. 6 finishing nails
Belt sander
Radial arm saw
Band saw
Ruler
Hammer
Drill bit
No. 10 plug cutter

CONSTRUCTION NOTES

Parts A, B, C, D, and G (Illus. 149)

Cut parts A (side), C (bottom), and G (center board) from $^3/_4$-inch birch plywood. Cut the dado and rabbet joints, as required, with a table saw or a radial arm saw. Part D (top) should be cut from solid birch.

Once pieces A, C, D, and G are cut to size, glue and nail them together with No. 6 finishing nails. Part D should be screwed to part A with $1^1/_4'' \times$ No. 10 flathead wood screws. These screws should be plugged and then sanded. Part B (back) can be made of either $^1/_4$-inch birch plywood or the less expensive fir plywood. Cut it to size with a table saw.

Use No. 4 ring-shank nails to secure part B to parts A, C, D, and G (body).

Parts P, Q, and R (Illus. 150)

See page 42 before building parts P (shelf adjustment bracket), Q (shelf support), and R (bracket insert); on these pages, the building instructions are outlined in detail. After cutting parts Q and R, screw them together so that they are flush on their tops. Attach part P to part A so that the brackets are flush on the front and flush with the rabbet joint on the back of part A. Use $^1/_4'' \times$ No. 10 flathead wood screws to attach part P.

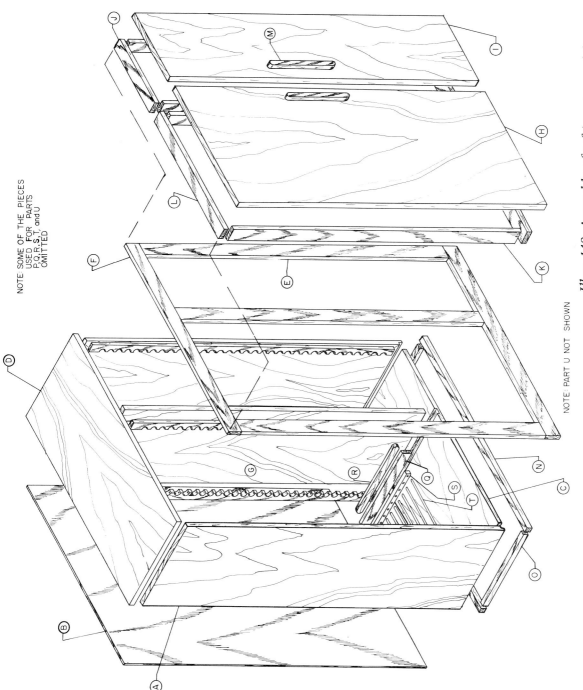

NOTE: SOME OF THE PIECES
USED FOR PARTS
P,Q,R,S,T, and U
OMITTED

NOTE: PART U NOT SHOWN

Illus. 148. Assembly of refrigerator and freezer.

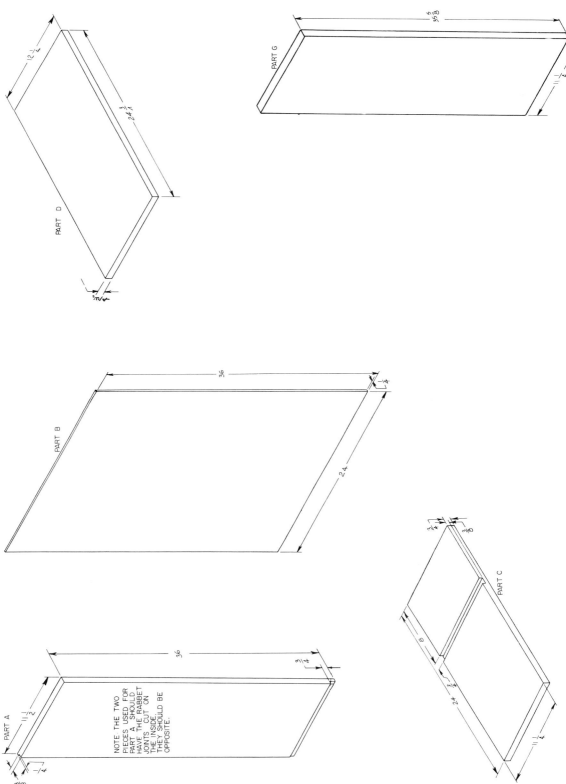

Illus. 149. Parts A, B, C, D, and G.

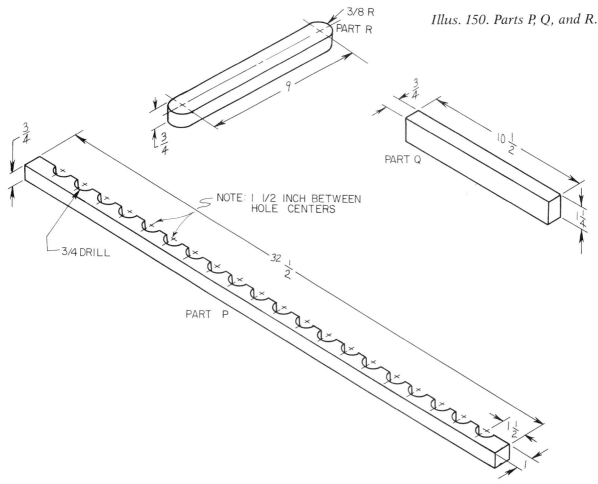

Illus. 150. Parts P, Q, and R.

3/8 R
PART R

9

3/4

PART Q

10 1/2

3/4

1 1/4

3/4

NOTE: 1 1/2 INCH BETWEEN
HOLE CENTERS

3/4 DRILL

32 1/2

PART P

1 1/2

1

Parts S, T, and U (Illus. 151)

Cut out part S (shelf side) with the table saw. Holding both pieces of part S that will be used for the same shelf, drill them with a twist bit and a drill press. Holding them together will assure perfect alignment of part T (shelf rod). Cut parts T and U (freezer shelf rod). Glue parts T and U into part S (shelf side) so that they are flush on the outside. These shelves should rest on part Q (shelf support).

Parts E and F (Illus. 152)

Cut part F (horizontal facing) first and use 1¼″ × No. 10 flathead wood screws to fasten it to parts A (side), C (bottom), and D (top). The facing should be flush on the outside of the refrigerator with freezer.

PART T
3/8 DOWEL, 12 1/2 LONG

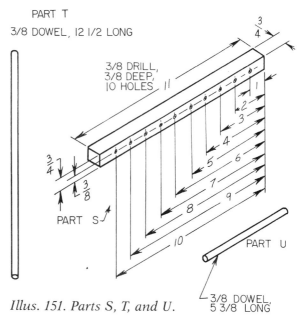

3/4

3/8 DRILL,
3/8 DEEP,
10 HOLES 11

1
2
3
4
5 6
7
8 9
10

3/4

3/8

PART S

PART U

3/8 DOWEL,
5 3/8 LONG

Illus. 151. Parts S, T, and U.

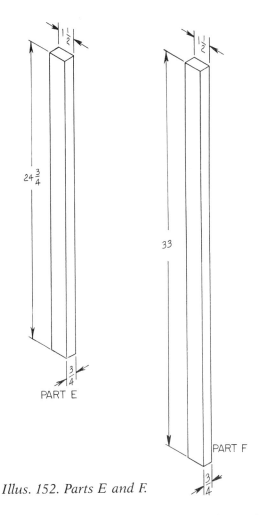

Illus. 152. Parts E and F.

Next, cut part E (vertical facing) to length. Cut each vertical facing individually to ensure a more exact fit. Screw them on; use a No. 10 plug cutter to fill the holes, and sand smooth.

Parts H, I, J, K, L, and M (Illus. 153 and 154)

Start the door by gluing up parts H (refrigerator door front) and I (freezer door front) from solid birch. Once they are glued, square the doors with a jointer and a table saw. Cut parts J (freezer door horizontal moulding) and L (refrigerator door horizontal moulding) to their correct sizes with the table saw. Glue and screw these parts from the front of parts H and I so that

parts L and J are flush on the outside of H and I. Fill the holes with plugs and then sand flush. Cut part K (freezer and refrigerator vertical moulding) to fit and attach in the same manner. Also screw part L to part K and part J to part K at the corners. Plug these parts; then sand them flush. Mount part E to the door with brass butt hinges so that the hinges are on the outside of the freezer.

Parts N and O (Illus. 155)

Cut parts N and O (base) with a table saw and attach them to the bottom of the refrigerator with freezer with 1¼″ × No. 10 flathead wood screws.

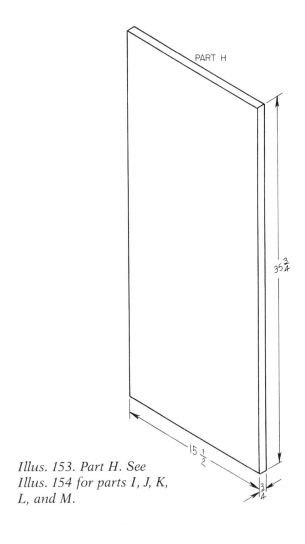

Illus. 153. Part H. See Illus. 154 for parts I, J, K, L, and M.

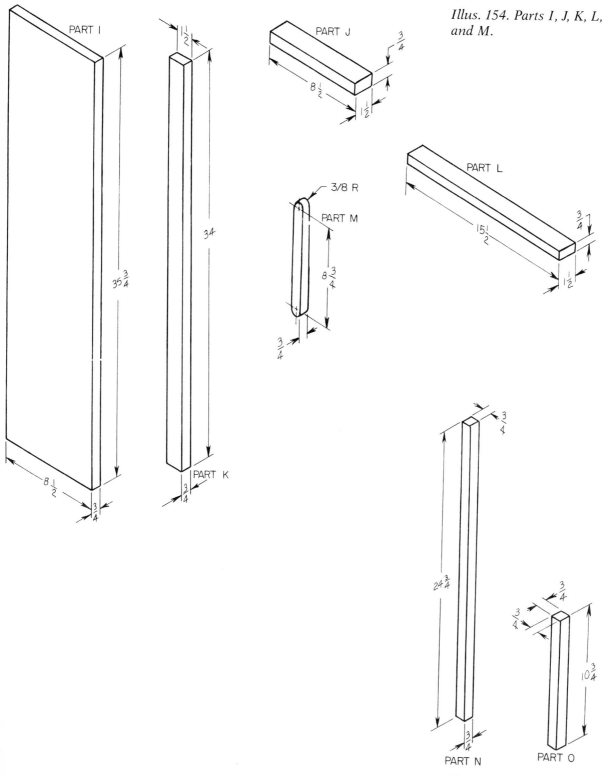

Illus. 154. Parts I, J, K, L, and M.

Illus. 155. Parts N and O.

Puzzles

Illus. 156.

CONSTRUCTION NOTES

The puzzles have different shapes and sizes; therefore, listing specific sizes would be impractical. The outside dimensions of your puzzles are not critical and can vary.

The puzzles can be made from two pieces of ¼-inch birch or oak plywood. Other veneered plywoods are also available, but usually at higher prices. Using plywood instead of solid wood helps prevent the narrow areas on the puzzle from breaking. Use a jigsaw to cut the pieces.

Parts A, B, and C (Illus. 157)

Lay out the shape of the puzzle on part B (outline). Drill a small hole (the size depends on the jigsaw blade you are using) in part B. Place the blade in the hole and then into the machine. Cut out the shape and remove the blade. Glue parts B and C together and cut the sides so that they appear as one board. Sand the edges of B and C (back). Paint part A (puzzle parts) as desired and stain parts B and C.

The puzzles shown in Illus. 158–175 are full size.

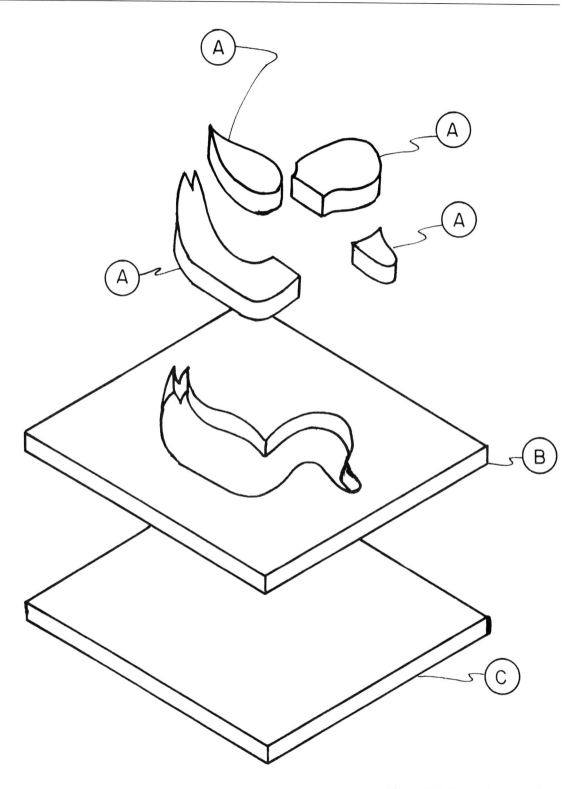

Illus. 157. Parts A, B, and C.

Illus. 158. Dog puzzle.

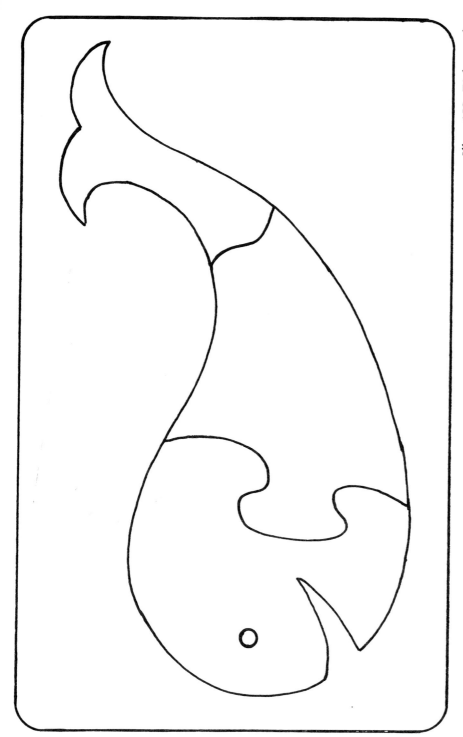

Illus. 159. Fish puzzle.

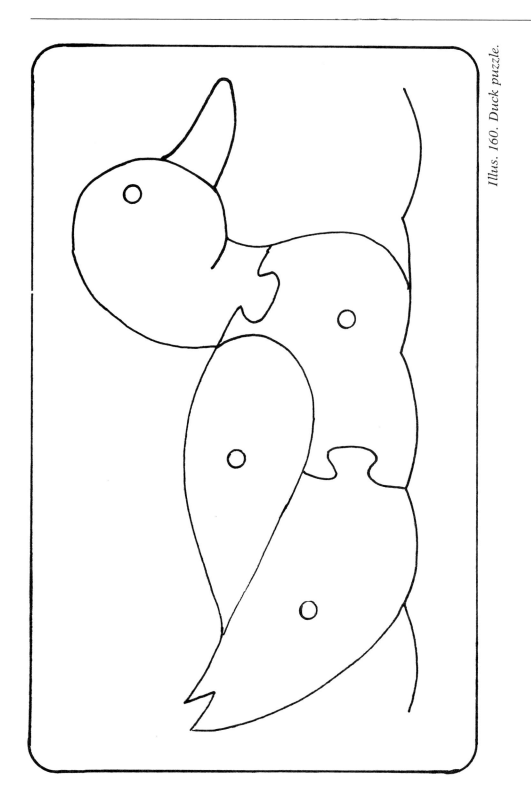

Illus. 160. Duck puzzle.

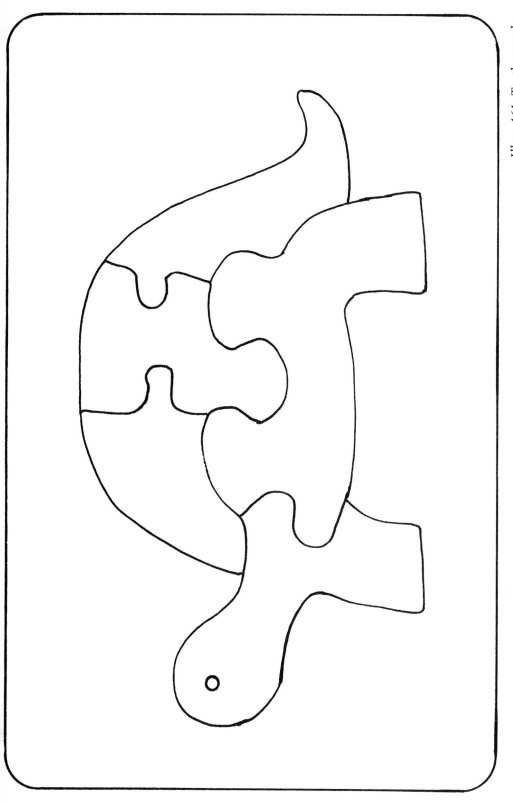

Illus. 162. Goose puzzle.

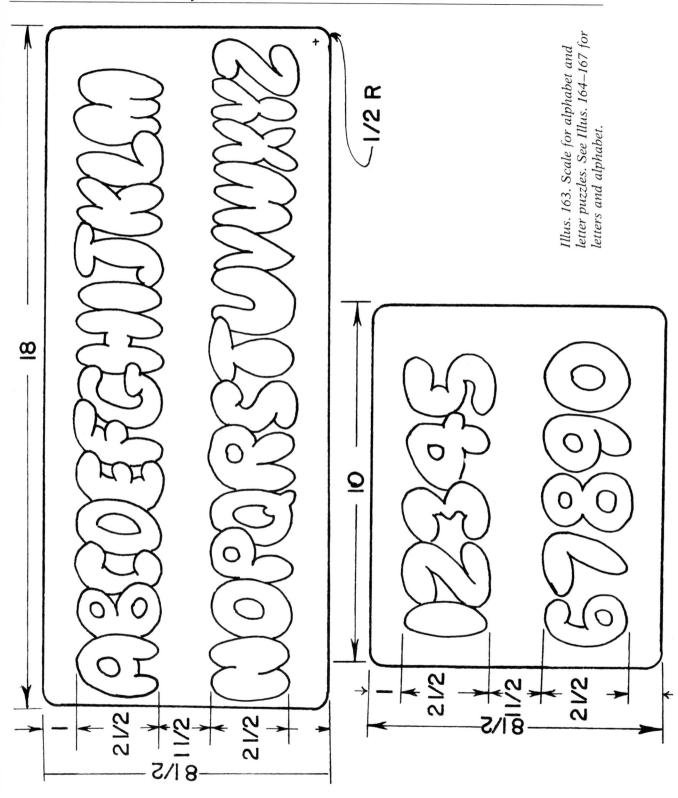

Illus. 163. Scale for alphabet and letter puzzles. See Illus. 164–167 for letters and alphabet.

Illus. 164. Letters A through J.

Illus. 165. Letters K through S.

Illus. 166. Letters T through Z.

Illus. 167. Numbers 0 through 9.

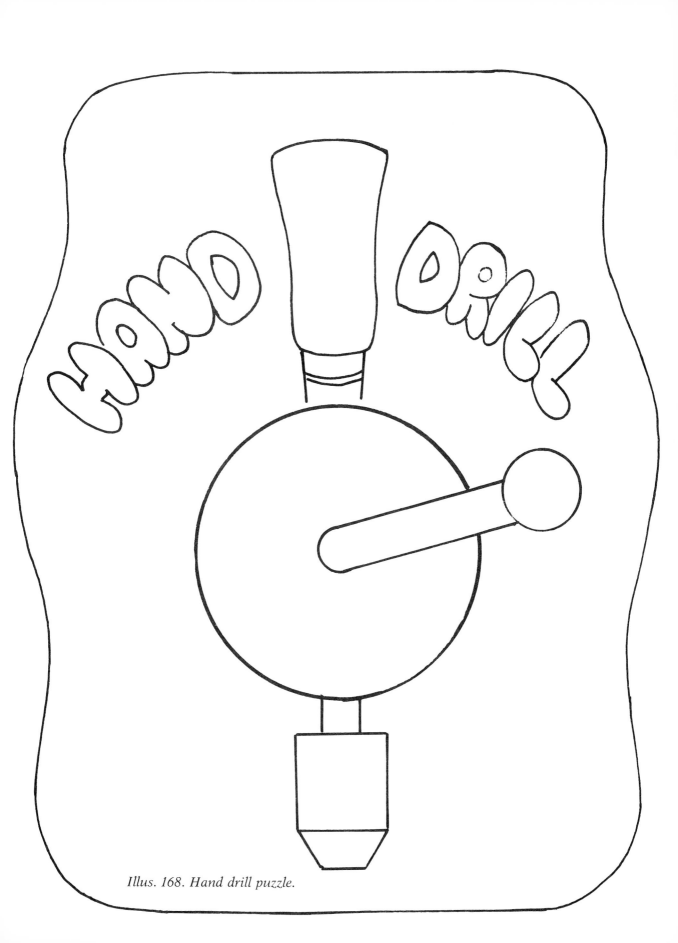

Illus. 168. Hand drill puzzle.

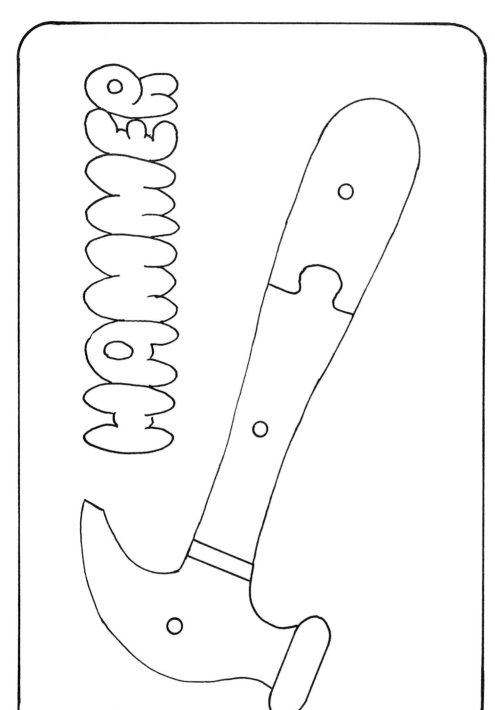

Illus. 170. Plane puzzle.

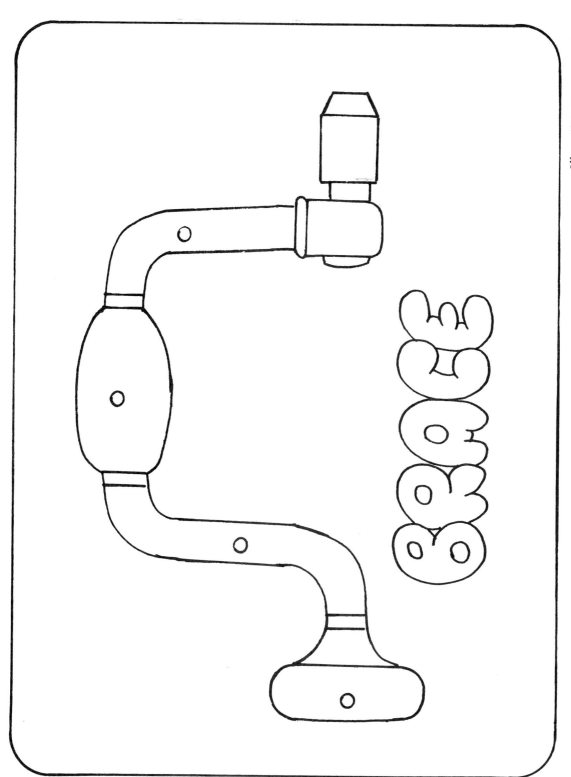

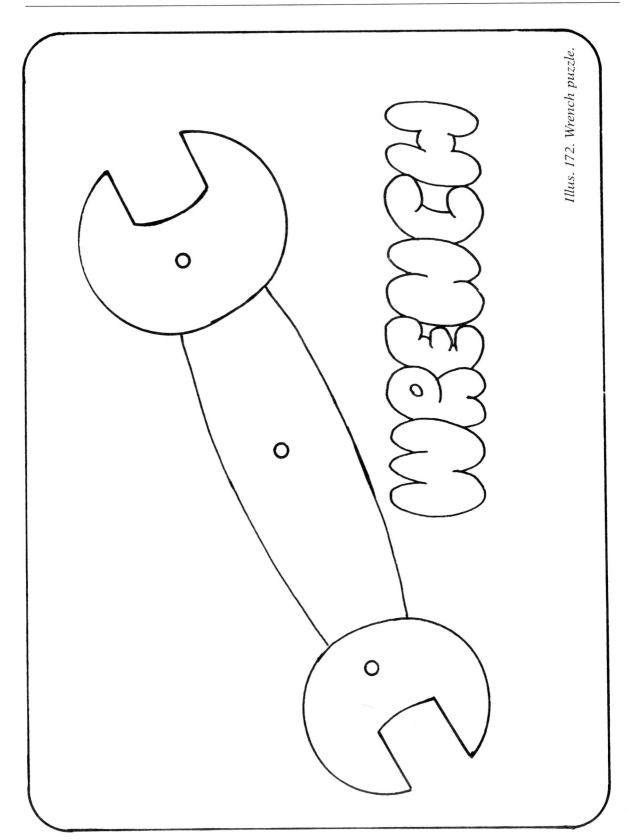

Illus. 172. Wrench puzzle.

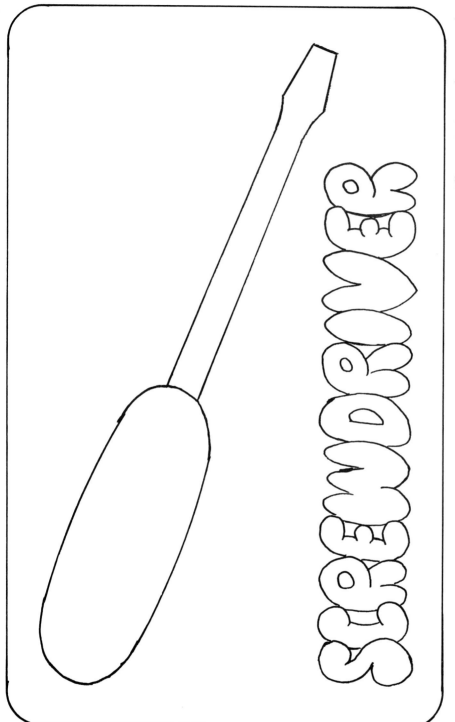

Illus. 173. Screwdriver puzzle.

Illus. 174. Saw puzzle.

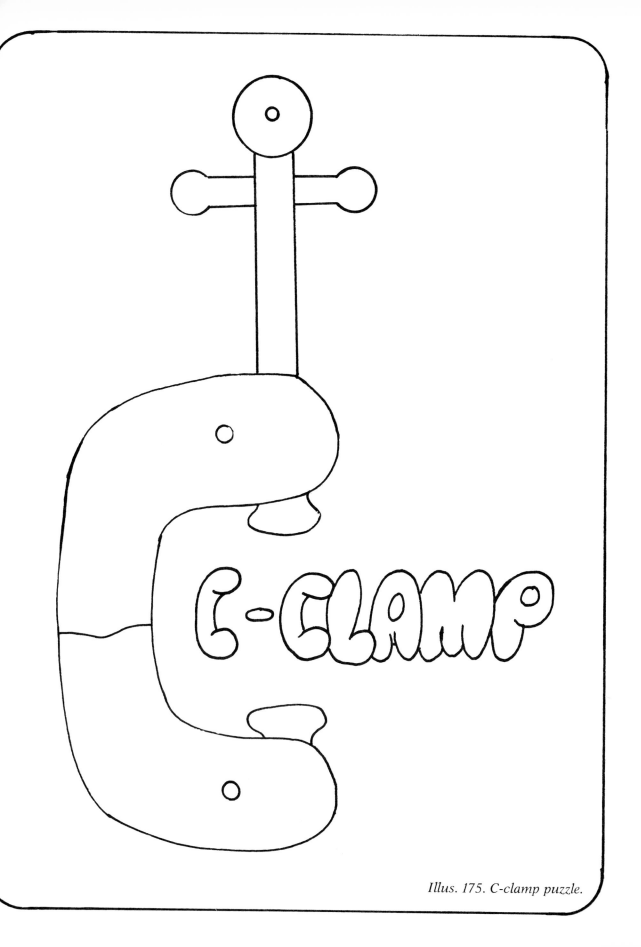

Illus. 175. C-clamp puzzle.

Penny Pool

Illus. 176.

Key to Assembly Shown in Illus. 177

LETTER	NUMBER REQUIRED	PART	SIZE
A	1	Bottom	16¾ × 10½ × ¾"
B	2	Side	16¾ × ⅝ × ½"
C	2	End	9 × ⅝ × ½"
D	8	Post	¼" dowel, 1¼" long

TOOLS AND SUPPLIES

Table saw   Drill press
Hammer   Twist bit
Forstner bit   Ruler
Try square   Glue

HOW TO PLAY

To play, place a penny on the starting spot as shown in Illus. 178. One player should start by flipping the penny with his finger or thumb towards the hole on the opponent's end. Each player gets one flip of the penny per turn. If the penny goes between the posts and in the hole, two points are scored. If the penny goes in the hole from the sides, one point is scored. The game is usually ten points.

I have found that penny pool is a lot of fun for anyone eight years old or older.

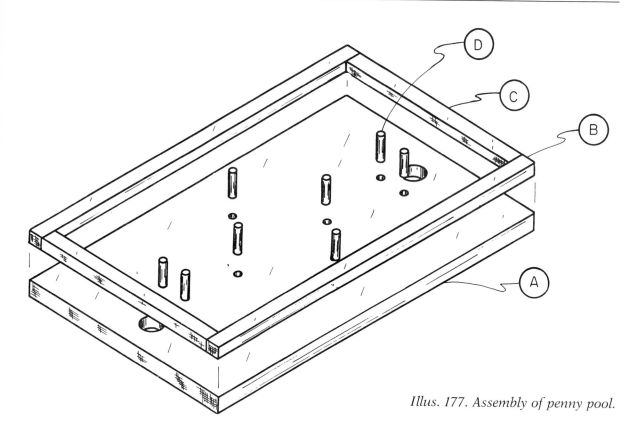

Illus. 177. Assembly of penny pool.

CONSTRUCTION NOTES

Part A (Illus. 178)

Part A (bottom) can be made from a variety of materials. When penny pools are made for large groups, such as school groups or scouts, ½-inch plywood should be used. One sheet of plywood will make 20 penny pools. Formica™ tops like those used on kitchen cabinets are excellent surfaces for the penny to slide on. When a kitchen sink is installed, the part of the counter top that is cut out will usually make one or two penny pools.

Regardless of the material, cut part A to size with a table saw or radial arm saw. Lay out the hole with a try square and ruler and drill the large hole that the penny drops through with a Forstner bit, and the smaller holes with a twist bit.

Parts B and C (Illus. 179)

Cut Parts B (side) and C (end) out of hardwood. Softwood, such as pine, tends to wear out easily as the penny hits the sides. Glue and/or screw the sides to Part A so that the edges of the sides and ends are flush with the outside edges of the bottom.

Part D (Illus. 180)

Cut part D to length with a coping saw or a table saw. Glue these posts into part A so that they are flush on the bottom of part A.

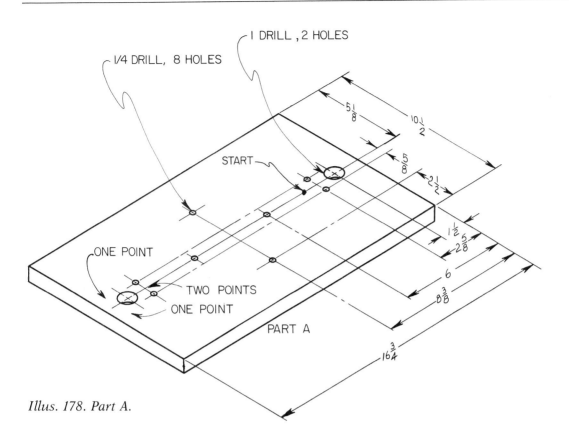

I DRILL , 2 HOLES

1/4 DRILL, 8 HOLES

$5\frac{1}{8}$

$10\frac{1}{2}$

START

$\frac{5}{8}$

$2\frac{1}{2}$

$1\frac{1}{2}$

$2\frac{5}{8}$

6

$8\frac{3}{8}$

ONE POINT

TWO POINTS

ONE POINT

PART A

$16\frac{3}{4}$

Illus. 178. Part A.

Illus. 179. Parts B and C.

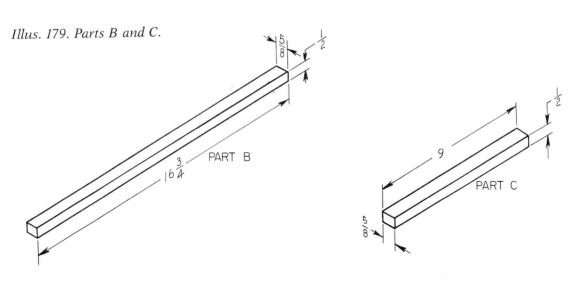

$\frac{5}{8}$ $\frac{1}{2}$

$\frac{1}{2}$

9

PART B

PART C

$16\frac{3}{4}$

$\frac{5}{8}$

1/4 DOWEL , 1 1/4 LONG

PART D

Illus. 180. Part D.

Skittles

Key to Assembly Shown in Illus. 182

LETTER	NUMBER REQUIRED	PART	SIZE
A	1	Bottom	$31^7/_8 \times 15^3/_4 \times {}^1/_2''$
B	2	Side	$31 \times 3 \times {}^1/_2''$
C	1	Solid end	$14^1/_4 \times 3 \times {}^1/_2''$
D	1	End (2 "gates")	$14^1/_4 \times 3 \times {}^1/_2''$
E	1	End (3 "gates")	$14^1/_4 \times 3 \times {}^1/_2''$
F	4	Single "gate"	$5 \times 3 \times {}^1/_2''$
G	1	Starting end	$14^1/_4 \times 3 \times {}^1/_2''$
H	1	Center board	$3^1/_2 \times 3 \times {}^1/_2''$
I	9	Pin	${}^1/_2''$ dowel, $2^1/_2''$ long
J	4	Top (hand)	$2 \times 2 \times {}^3/_4''$
K	4	Top (stem)	${}^1/_4''$ dowel, $2^1/_2''$ long

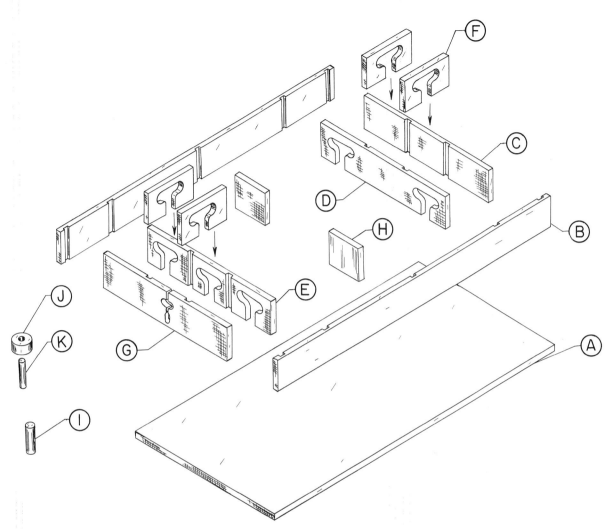

Illus. 182. Assembly of skittles.

TOOLS AND SUPPLIES

Table saw	Jigsaw or band saw
Radial arm saw	Try square
Drill press	1" × No. 8
Forstner bit	combination drill
No. 8 plug cutter	Glue
Hole saw	1" × No. 8 flathead
Jointer	wood screw
Dado head	

HOW TO PLAY

In this version of skittles, pins are set up;
each pin has an assigned number. This
number represents the number of points
that particular pin is worth. Any number of
players can play; each player takes a turn
spinning the top. The top spins and travels
through the maze of gates, knocking down
pins as it goes.

Each player can keep his own score by
adding the points he gets for the pins he
knocked down. The winner is the one who
reaches a specific score, such as 100 or 200,
first.

CONSTRUCTION NOTES

Part A (Illus. 183)

Part A (bottom) may be made out of either birch plywood or solid birch. I use ½-inch birch plywood, which is light, but ¾-inch birch will work equally well. Cut part A out with a table saw.

Parts B, C, D, E, F, G, and H (Illus. 184 and 185)

Start these parts by first planing enough stock to the required thickness on a jointer or a planer. Joint one edge on the jointer; then rip all the stock to the correct width. Lay out the dadoes and cut them on a radial arm saw or table saw with a dado head. Before cutting the dadoes, make a practice cut on a scrap board to make sure you have a firm-fitting joint.

Next, drill out the holes for the doors ("gates") on parts D (end), E (end), and F (single "gate"). Use a jigsaw or band saw to finish cutting out the doors. On part G (starting end), use the same procedure.

Once all the parts have been sanded, glue part F into parts C (solid end) and D and into parts E and G. Next, glue parts C, D, E, G, and H (center board) into part B (side). Glue these into the dadoes and use a 1 × 8″ flathead wood screw to ensure that these parts stay together. Cover the wood screw with a wood plug made with a No. 8 plug cutter and a drill press.

Once parts B, C, D, E, F, G, and H are assembled into one unit, center this unit on part A. Attach this unit with 1″ × No. 8 wood screws from the bottom into the sides and ends. Make sure that part H also has a wood screw, fastening it from the bottom.

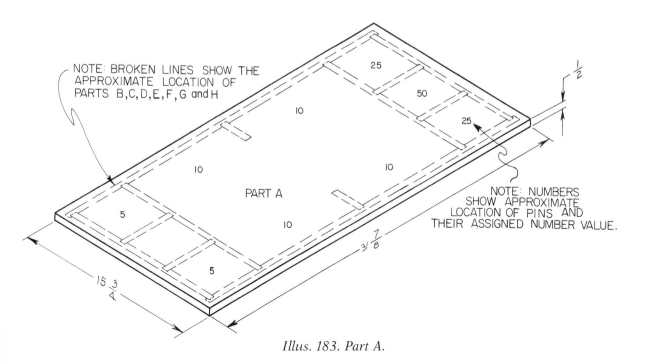

Illus. 183. Part A.

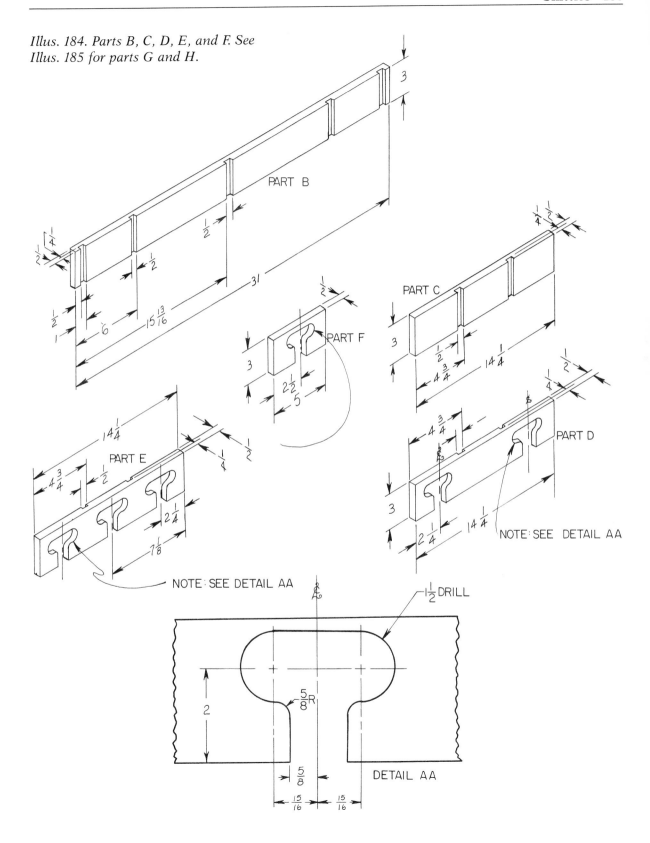

*Illus. 184. Parts B, C, D, E, and F. See
Illus. 185 for parts G and H.*

PART B

PART C

PART F

PART E

PART D

NOTE: SEE DETAIL AA

NOTE: SEE DETAIL AA

$1\frac{1}{2}$ DRILL

$\frac{5}{8}$ R

DETAIL AA

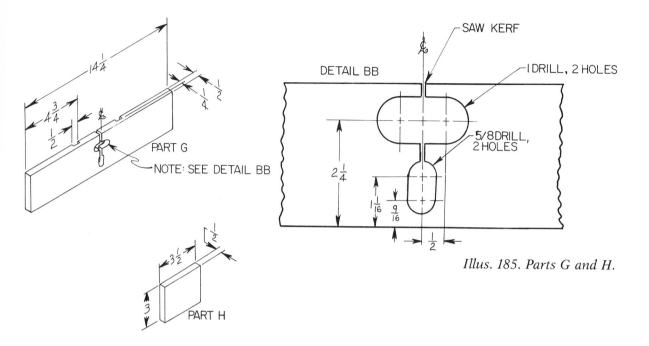

Illus. 185. Parts G and H.

Parts I, J, and K (Illus. 186)

Use a drill press and a hole saw to make part J (top head). Cut part K (top stem) from a dowel rod. Glue part K into part J so that they are flush on top. Make sure that part J is at the right height and can go through the "gates." The bottom part of part K can be rounded by hand or can be sharpened to a sharp point with a pencil sharpener. Experimenting with different-shaped ends will result in tops that perform differently.

Part I (pin) is simply a ½-inch dowel rod cut to the correct length. This cut must be square so that the pin will stand easily. Part I can also be turned on a lathe to resemble a small bowling pin or any original shape.

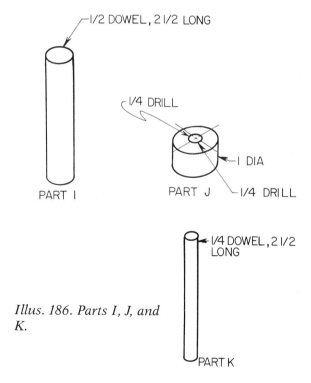

Illus. 186. Parts I, J, and K.

Biplane

Illus. 187. See page B of the color section for a look at the biplane in full color.

Key to Assembly Shown in Illus. 188

LETTER	NUMBER REQUIRED	PART	SIZE
A	1	Fuselage	$11 \times 3 \times 5''$
B	1	Upper wing	$14 \times 3^{1}/_{2} \times {^1}/_{2}''$
C	1	Lower wing	$14 \times 3^{1}/_{2} \times {^1}/_{2}''$
D	1	Engine	$2^{1}/_{4} \times 2^{1}/_{4} \times {^3}/_{4}''$
E	1	Propeller	$7 \times 1 \times {^3}/_{8}''$
F	1	Propeller cap	$^{3}/_{4}''$ dowel, $^{5}/_{8}''$ long
G	8	Engine cylinder heads	$^{1}/_{2}''$ dowel, $1''$ long
H	1	Propeller shaft	$^{1}/_{4}''$ dowel, $2''$ long
I	1	Windshield	$1^{1}/_{2} \times {^3}/_{8} \times {^1}/_{2}''$
J	1	Headrest	$1^{1}/_{2} \times {^3}/_{4} \times 1''$
K	1	Rear wing	$6 \times 2 \times {^1}/_{2}''$
L	1	Rear wing lock	$^{1}/_{4}''$ dowel, $2^{1}/_{2}''$ long
M	1	Back wheel	$^{13}/_{16} \times {^{13}/_{16}} \times {^1}/_{2}''$
N	1	Rear wheel support	$^{1}/_{4}''$ dowel, $1^{1}/_{2}''$ long
O	1	Front wheel support	$3^{3}/_{4} \times 2^{1}/_{8} \times {^3}/_{4}''$
P	1	Front wheel	$1^{1}/_{2} \times 1^{1}/_{2} \times {^3}/_{4}''$
Q	1	Front axle	$^{1}/_{4}''$ dowel, $5^{3}/_{8}''$ long
R	8	Wing brace	$^{1}/_{4}''$ dowel, $4^{1}/_{4}''$ long

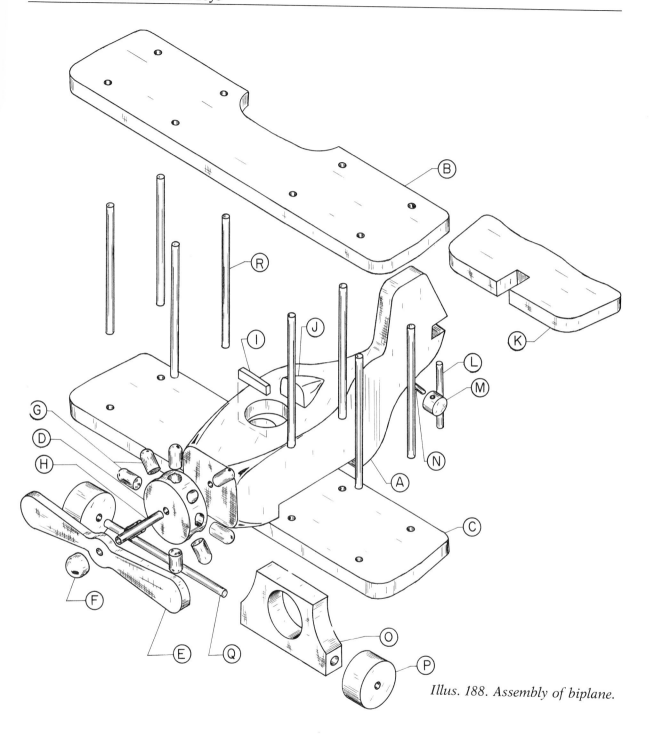

Illus. 188. Assembly of biplane.

TOOLS AND SUPPLIES

Band saw   Jointer
Drill press   Ruler
Try square   Forstner bits
Wood file   ¼″ × No. 10
Twist bits   combination drill
Hole saw   ¼″ × No. 10 flathead
Glue   wood screws
Coping saw   Disc sander
Table saw

CONSTRUCTION NOTES

Part A (Illus. 189)

Cut the shape of part A (fuselage) with a band saw. See pages 43–45 for instructions on making the cut. Drill the holes for the seat section with Forstner bits and a drill press. Drill the holes that parts H and N will fit into.

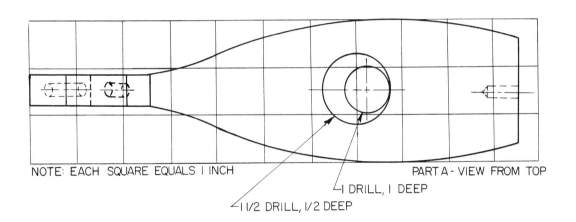

NOTE: EACH SQUARE EQUALS 1 INCH   PART A - VIEW FROM TOP

└1 DRILL, 1 DEEP

└11/2 DRILL, 1/2 DEEP

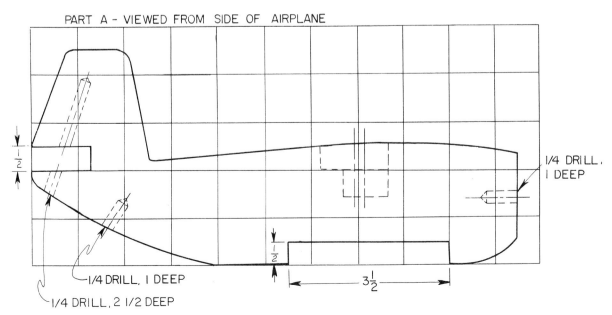

PART A - VIEWED FROM SIDE OF AIRPLANE

1/4 DRILL,
1 DEEP

1/4 DRILL, 1 DEEP

1/4 DRILL, 2 1/2 DEEP

3½

Illus. 189. Part A.

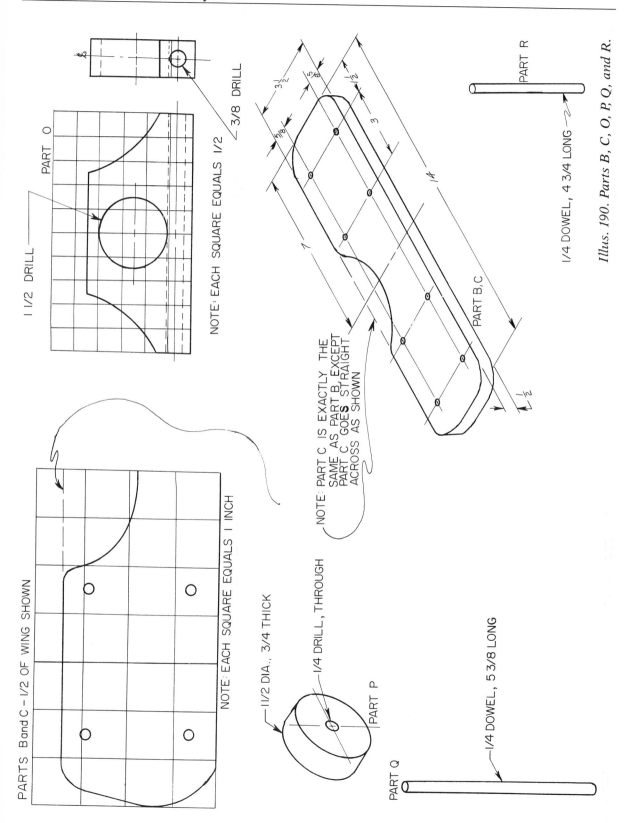

PART O

¢

3/8 DRILL

1 1/2 DRILL

NOTE: EACH SQUARE EQUALS 1/2

PART B,C

3½

⅝

⅝

½

3

1¼

1

½

NOTE: PART C IS EXACTLY THE
SAME AS PART B EXCEPT
PART C GOES STRAIGHT
ACROSS AS SHOWN

PART R

1/4 DOWEL, 4 3/4 LONG

Illus. 190. Parts B, C, O, P, Q, and R.

PARTS B and C - 1/2 OF WING SHOWN

NOTE: EACH SQUARE EQUALS 1 INCH

1 1/2 DIA., 3/4 THICK

1/4 DRILL, THROUGH

PART P

PART Q

1/4 DOWEL, 5 3/8 LONG

Parts B, C, O, P, Q, and R
(Illus. 192 and 193)

Plane enough stock for part B (upper wing), C (lower wing), and K (rear wing). Part K should be made later (see page 174). Cut the shapes for parts B and C with a table saw; then round the corners with a band saw. Hold these two parts together, and drill the holes that part R (wing braces) will fit into.

Cut part O (front wheel support) out with a band saw and drill the holes with a drill press. Attach part O to part C, using 1¼″ × No. 10 flathead wood screws from the top of part C. Part O should be centered from side to side and approximately an inch from the front of part C.

Cut part R to length and glue the wing braces into parts B and C so that they are flush on the top of B and the bottom of C. Attach part A to part C with 1¼″ × No. 10 flathead wood screws so that part A is centered from side to side on part C. Cut part P (front wheel) out with a hole saw and a drill press. Cut part Q (front axle) to length, slide it through part O, and glue part P on so that P and Q are flush on the outside.

Parts I and J (Illus. 191)

Cut out part I (windshield) with a coping saw. Attach it to part A with glue. Part I should be approximately ⅛ inch in front of the large hole drilled for the seat, and centered from side to side. Cut part J (headrest) out with a coping saw; glue and nail it to part A. Part J should be centered from side to side and should be ¼ inch behind the hole that is used for the seat.

Parts D, E, F, G, and H
(Illus. 192 and 193)

Cut part H (propeller shaft) to length and glue it into part A so that it protrudes by approximately 1½ inch. Using a hole saw, cut out part D (engine) and drill the holes for part G (engine cylinder press) on a drill press. Sand the round ends on part G on a disc sander; make sure the dowel is long enough to be safely used. Then cut part G to length. Glue part G into part D so that part G protrudes by approximately ½ inch. Slide part D over part H and glue it onto part H so that it touches part I.

Cut part E (propeller) from a thin piece of stock with a band saw. Make part F (propeller cap) in the same manner that part G was made, and drill the hole in the end of part F with a drill press. Slide part E onto part H, making sure it turns smoothly, and glue part F onto the end of part H.

Illus. 191. Parts I and J.

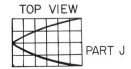

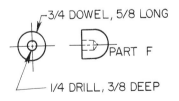

-3/4 DOWEL, 5/8 LONG
PART F
1/4 DRILL, 3/8 DEEP

TOP VIEW

PART J

NOTE: EACH SQUARE EQUALS 1/4

ROUND TO 1/4 R

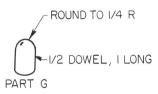

1/2 DOWEL, 1 LONG

PART G

Illus. 192. Parts F and G. See Illus. 193 for parts D, E, and H.

Illus. 193. Parts D, E, and H.

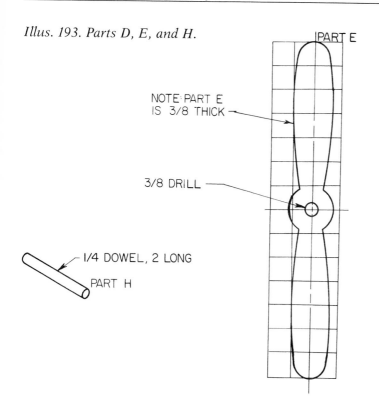

NOTE: PART E
IS 3/8 THICK

PART E

3/8 DRILL

1/4 DOWEL, 2 LONG
PART H

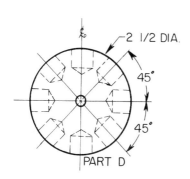

2 1/2 DIA.

45°

45°

PART D

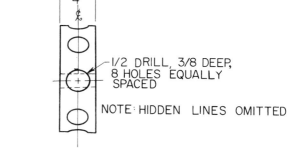

3/4

1/2 DRILL, 3/8 DEEP,
8 HOLES EQUALLY
SPACED

NOTE: HIDDEN LINES OMITTED

Part K, L, M, and N (Illus. 194 and 195)

Cut part K out with a band saw. Cut out parts L (rear wing lock) and N (near wheel support). Slide part K onto part A. Drill the hole through parts A and K, and glue part L into this hole. Cut part L off on the bottom, making it flush with part A. Cut part M (back wheel) out with a drill press and hand saw, and drill the required hole. Glue part N into part A, and part M onto part A.

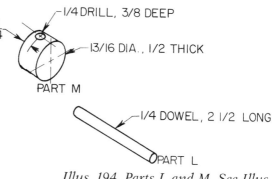

1/4

1/4 DRILL, 3/8 DEEP

13/16 DIA., 1/2 THICK

PART M

1/4 DOWEL, 2 1/2 LONG

PART L

Illus. 194. Parts L and M. See Illus. 195 for parts K and N.

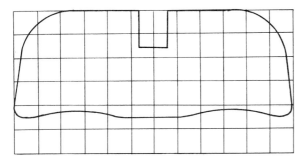

PART K   NOTE: THICKNESS IS 1/2 INCH
                 EACH SQUARE EQUALS 1/2 INCH

1/4 DOWEL, 1 1/2 LONG

PART N

Illus. 195. Parts K and N.

Piper Cub

Illus. 196. See page B of the color section for a look at the Piper Cub in full color.

Key to Assembly Shown in Illus. 197

LETTER	NUMBER REQUIRED	PART	SIZE
A	1	Fuselage	$3^3/_4 \times 2^3/_4 \times 14^1/_2''$
B	1	Main wing	$20 \times 3 \times {}^1/_2''$
C	4	Wing support bracket	$1^3/_8 \times {}^9/_{16} \times {}^7/_{16}''$
D	4	Wing support	$^1/_4''$ dowel, $6^1/_2''$ long
E	2	Wheel support	$^3/_4''$ dowel, $3^1/_2''$ long
F	2	Front wheel	$1^5/_8 \times 1^5/_8 \times {}^1/_4''$
G	2	Wheel cap	$^3/_4''$ dowel, $1^1/_2''$ long
H	2	Front axle	$^1/_4''$ dowel, $1^1/_2''$ long
I	1	Propeller	$7 \times 1^1/_8 \times {}^1/_4''$
J	1	Propeller cap	$^3/_4''$ dowel, $^1/_2''$ long
K	1	Propeller shaft	$^1/_4''$ dowel, $1^1/_4''$ long
L	1	Back wing	$7 \times 1^7/_8 \times {}^7/_{16}''$
M	1	Inner brace	$^1/_4''$ dowel, 2'' long
N	1	Back wheel	$^3/_4 \times {}^3/_4 \times {}^1/_2''$
O	1	Back wheel support	$^1/_4''$ dowel, $1^1/_2''$ long

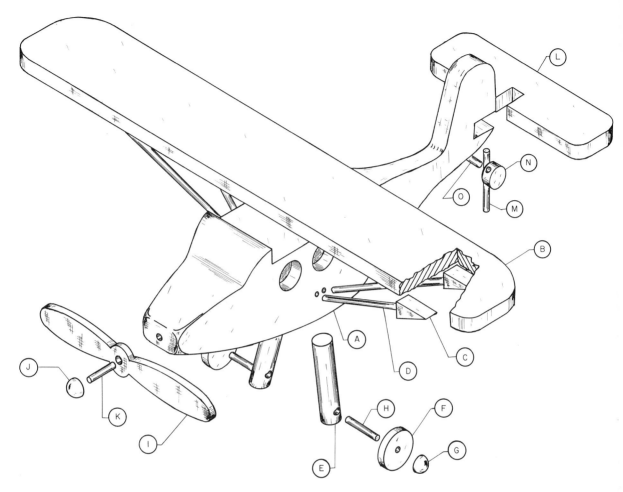

Illus. 197. Assembly of Piper Cub.

TOOLS AND SUPPLIES

Band saw
Table saw
Try square
Wood file
Twist bit
No. 10 plug cutter
Hand-screw clamp
1¼" × No.10
    combination drill
    and countersink

Drill press
Coping saw
Ruler
Forstner bit
Hole saw
Electric hand drill
Glue
1¼" × No. 10 flathead
    wood screws

CONSTRUCTION NOTES

Part A (Illus. 198)

Pages 43–45 discuss how to build part A (fuselage). Once the shape has been cut out, use a Forstner bit and a drill press to drill out the window. Use a twist bit to drill the holes for parts D (wing support), K (propeller shaft), and M (inner brace). (See Illus. 199 for part D, Illus. 202 for part K, and Illus. 200 for part M.)

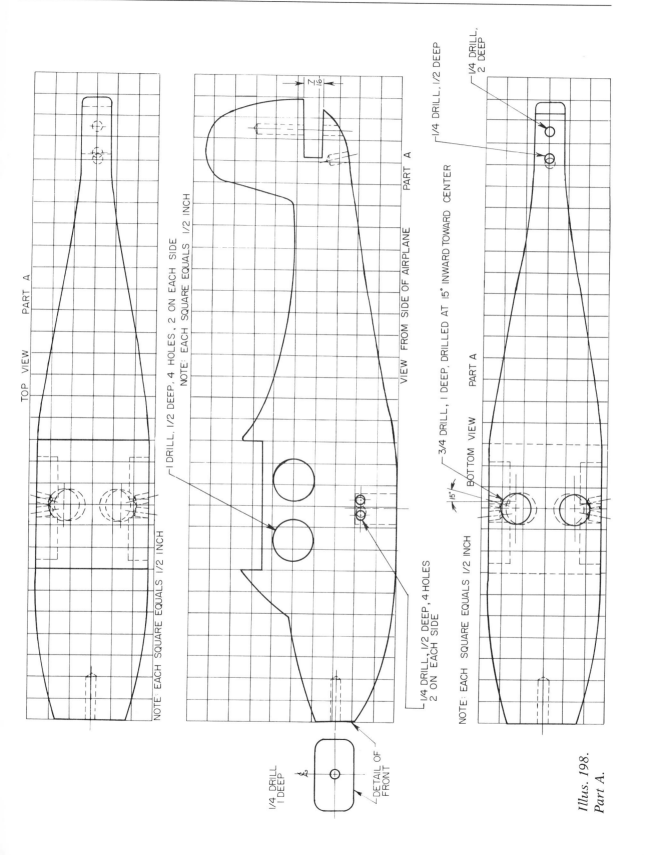

Illus. 198. Part A.

Drill the holes for part E (wheel support) with a spade bit or a Forstner bit. (See Illus. 201 for part E.) If you are making the Piper Cub with the pontoons, do not drill the holes for part E. Page 183 discusses how to make the pontoons.

Parts B, C, and D (Illus. 199)

Cut the dowel rod for part D (wing support). Plane or joint a board to the correct thickness for part B (main wing). Cut the shape of part B with a band saw. Cut part C (wing support bracket) on a band saw and use a drill press and twist bit to drill the required hole.

Center the main wing on part A (fuselage). Using two 1¼″ × No. 10 flathead wood screws, attach part B to part A. Cover these screws with wood plugs made with a No. 10 plug cutter on a drill press. Glue part D into part A and glue part C onto part D. Glue part C to part B so that part C is approximately ⅛ to ¼ of an inch away from the edge of the wing.

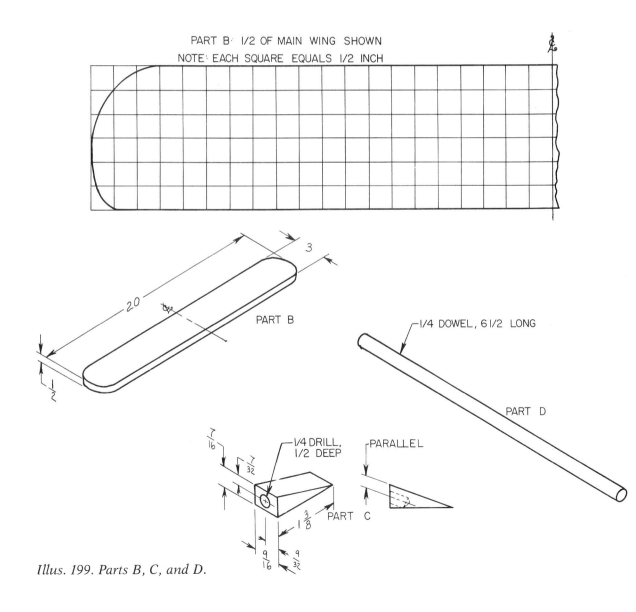

Illus. 199. Parts B, C, and D.

Parts L, M, N, and O (Illus. 200)

Cut parts O (back wheel support) and M (inner brace) to length. Using a hole saw and a drill press, make part N (back wheel). Cut part L (back wing) out with a band saw. Slide the back wing into the half-lap joint on part A. Use an electric hand drill or drill press to drill a hole through part A and into part L. Glue part M into this hole, locking part L onto part A. Cut the bottom of part M off so that it is flush with part A. Glue part N (back wheel) onto part O and part O into part A. There should be approximately ¼ of an inch between parts N and A.

Parts E, F, G, and H (Illus. 201)

These parts should *not* be made if you are equipping your plane with pontoons rather than wheels. Cut the dowels to length for parts E (wheel support) and H (front axle). Drill the hole through part E.

Glue part E into the plane so that the plane sits level.

Cut part H and glue it into the hole in part E. Use a hole saw to make part F (front wheel) from a thin piece of stock. Slide part F over part H. File and sand the end of a dowel rod to make part G (wheel cap). Holding part G in a hand-screw clamp, drill the required hole. Glue part G into part H, making sure that part F turns smoothly.

Parts I, J, and K (Illus. 202)

File and sand an end of a dowel rod round for part J (propeller cap). Drill the hole in part J with a twist bit and drill press. Cut part K (propeller shaft) to length and glue it into part A so that it protrudes by approximately ¾ of an inch. Cut part I (propeller) out with a band saw and drill the hole with a drill press. Slide part I over part K, and glue on part J, making sure that part I turns smoothly.

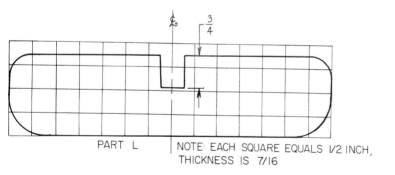

PART L   NOTE: EACH SQUARE EQUALS 1/2 INCH, THICKNESS IS 7/16

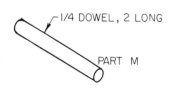

1/4 DOWEL, 2 LONG

PART M

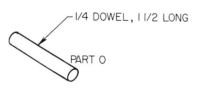

1/4 DOWEL, 1 1/2 LONG

PART O

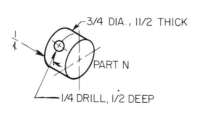

3/4 DIA., 1 1/2 THICK

PART N

1/4 DRILL, 1/2 DEEP

Illus. 200. Parts L, M, N, and O.

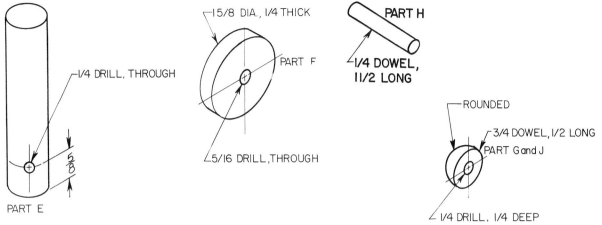

Illus. 201. Parts E, F, G, and H.

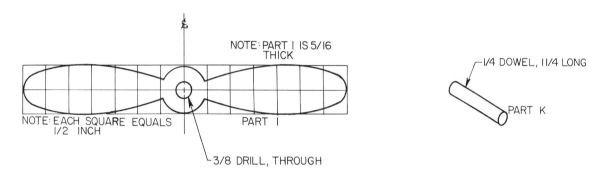

Illus. 202. Parts I and K. The drawing for part G in Illus. 201 also applies to part J.

PIPER CUB WITH PONTOONS

Illus. 203. See page C of the color section for a look at the Piper Cub with pontoons in full color.

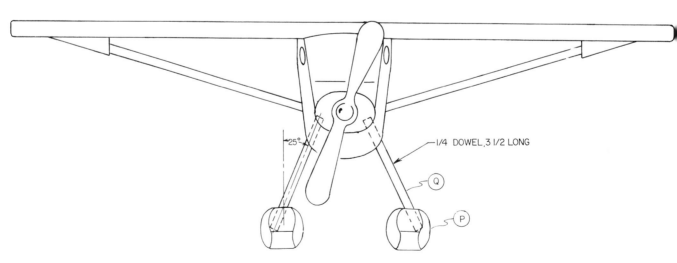

Illus. 204. Assembly of Piper   Cub with pontoons.

Key to Assembly Shown in Illus. 204

LETTER	NUMBER REQUIRED	PART	SIZE
P	2	Pontoon	$7 \times 1\frac{1}{2} \times 1\frac{1}{2}''$
Q	4	Pontoon support	$\frac{1}{4}''$ dowel, $3\frac{1}{2}''$ long

Parts A, P, and Q (Illus. 205)

Cut part P (pontoon) out on a band saw. Drill the holes for part Q (pontoon support) with an electric hand drill. Cut the dowel rods to length for part Q. Drill the four holes into part A (fuselage) at the approximate angle for part Q to fit into. Glue part Q into part A. Then glue part P onto part Q. Make sure the plane is parallel to the ground as seen from the front view. You can adjust the plane so that it is parallel to the ground by sliding part Q in or out of part A.

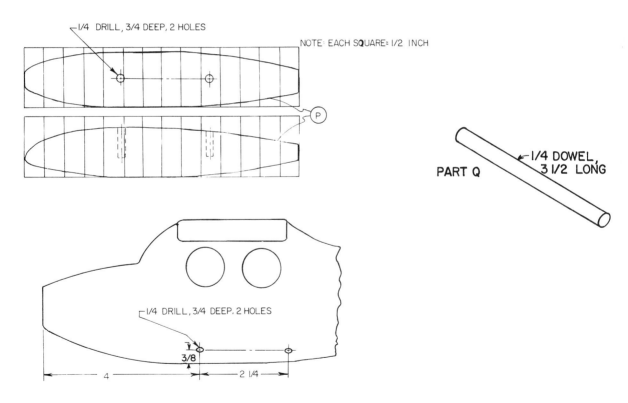

Illus. 205. Part Q. Part A (body of the fuselage) is also shown.

Helicopter

Illus. 206. See page C of the color section for a look at the helicopter in full color.

Key to Assembly Shown in Illus. 207

LETTER	NUMBER REQUIRED	PART	SIZE
A	1	Fuselage	$5 \times 4^{7}/_{8} \times 2^{3}/_{4}''$
B	1	Rotor	$1^{3}/_{4} \times {}^{3}/_{16} \times 16''$
C	2	Landing gear	$^{1}/_{2} \times {}^{3}/_{4} \times 6^{1}/_{2}''$
D	1	Rear rotor mount	$^{3}/_{4} \times 1^{1}/_{2} \times 1^{5}/_{8}''$
E	2	Rear rotor	$^{3}/_{16} \times {}^{5}/_{8} \times 4^{3}/_{4}''$
F	1	Rear rotor axle	$^{1}/_{4}''$ dowel, $1^{3}/_{8}''$ long
G	2	Frame	$^{1}/_{4}''$ dowel, $10^{1}/_{2}''$ long
H	4	Landing gear	$^{1}/_{4}''$ dowel, $3''$ long
I	1	Rotor bearing	$^{3}/_{4}''$ dowel, $1^{1}/_{2}''$ long
J	1	Rotor cap	$^{3}/_{4}''$ dowel, $^{3}/_{4}''$ long
K	1	Rotor axle	$^{1}/_{4}''$ dowel, $1^{1}/_{4}''$ long

Illus. 207. Assembly of helicopter.

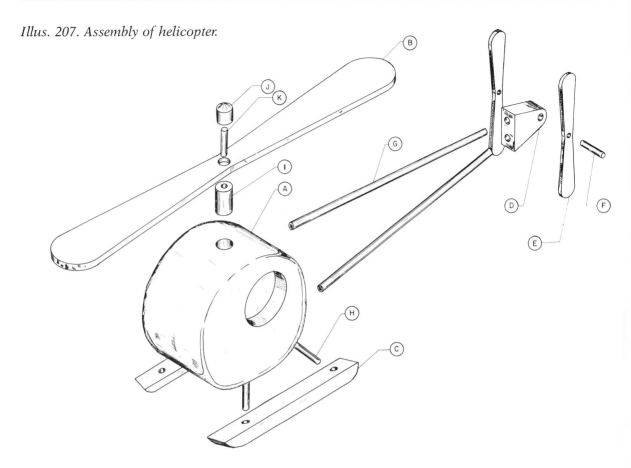

TOOLS AND SUPPLIES

Band saw	Belt sander
Drill press	Twist bits
Forstner bit	Wood rasp
Hammer	File
Table saw	Sandpaper

CONSTRUCTION NOTES

Part A (Illus. 208)

Lay out the pattern as seen from the side and cut out the shape of part A (fuselage) using a band saw. Drill the large hole for the window with a Forstner bit and drill press. Drill the other holes with a drill press and twist bits. Round the edges of part A with a wood rasp, file, and sandpaper.

Parts C and H (Illus. 209)

Rip a long piece of stock on the table saw for part C (landing gear). Use the band saw to cut the curves. Cut out part H (landing gear) and glue part H into part C and into part A. Set the helicopter on a flat surface and make sure it is sitting level as seen from the front and both sides.

Parts D, E, F, and G (Illus. 210)

Cut the dowel to length for part G (frame). Use a band saw to cut out part D (rear rotor mount) and drill the required holes with a drill press and twist bits. Plane enough stock for part E (rear rotor) and cut part E out on the band saw. Cut part F (rear rotor axle) to length. Glue part G into part A, leaving both pieces of part G protruding out of part A at the same distance.

Glue both pieces of G into part D. Slide part F through the hole in part D. Glue part

NOTE: EACH SQUARE EQUALS 1 INCH

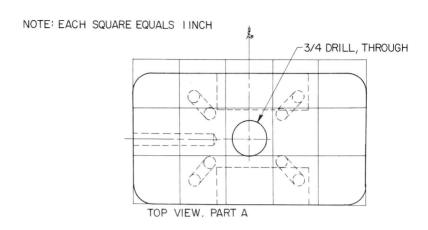

3/4 DRILL, THROUGH

TOP VIEW, PART A

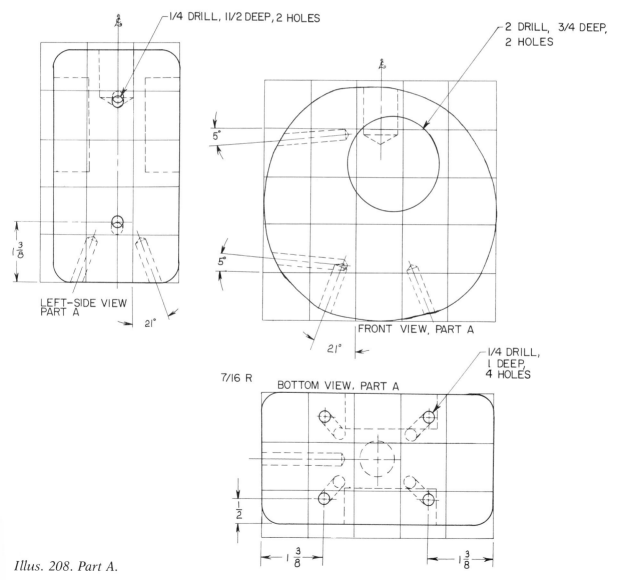

1/4 DRILL, 1 1/2 DEEP, 2 HOLES

2 DRILL, 3/4 DEEP, 2 HOLES

5°

5°

$1\frac{3}{8}$

LEFT-SIDE VIEW
PART A

21°

FRONT VIEW, PART A

21°

7/16 R

1/4 DRILL, 1 DEEP, 4 HOLES

BOTTOM VIEW, PART A

$\frac{1}{2}$

$1\frac{3}{8}$

$1\frac{3}{8}$

Illus. 208. Part A.

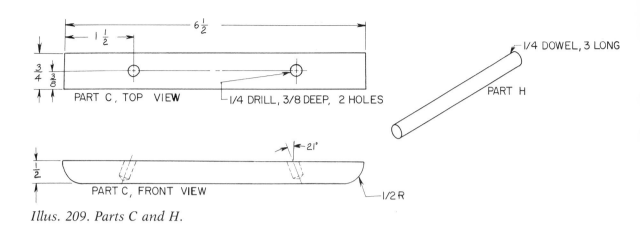

Illus. 209. Parts C and H.

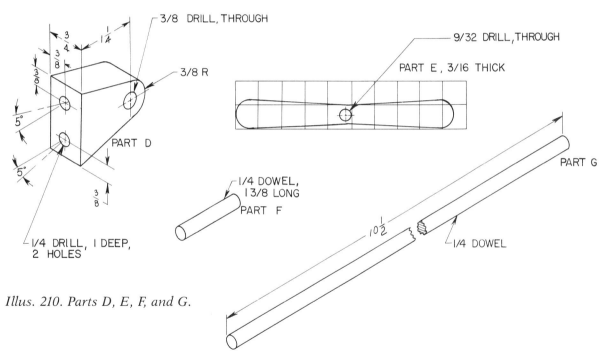

Illus. 210. Parts D, E, F, and G.

E onto part F on both sides so that parts E and F are flush on the outside.

Parts B, I, J, and K (Illus. 211)

Cut part I (rotor bearing) and drill the required hole on a drill press. Glue part I into part A so that part I protrudes out of part A by ½ inch. Cut part K (rotor axle) and glue it into part I so that it protrudes out of part I by approximately ¾ of an inch. Resaw or plane a piece of stock large enough to make part B (rotor). Cut the rotor out on a band saw and drill the hole with a twist bit and drill press.

Make the tapered section of part J with a belt sander and a long dowel rod. Then cut the dowel rod to the correct length for part J (rotor cap). Drill the hole in the end of part J; place part B onto part K and glue part J onto part K. Make sure that part B turns smoothly.

Illus. 211. Parts B, I, J, and K.

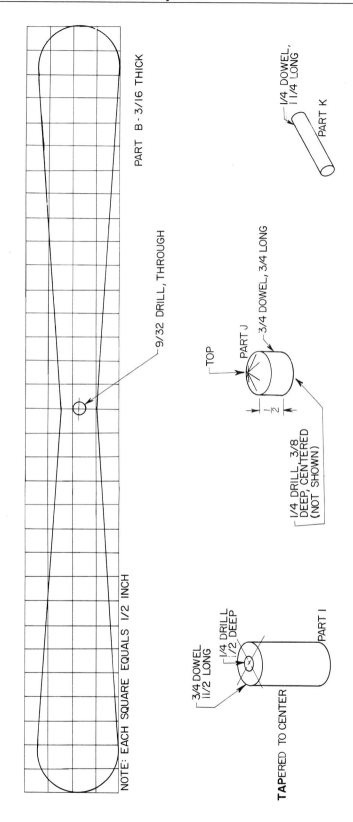

PART B - 3/16 THICK

9/32 DRILL, THROUGH

NOTE: EACH SQUARE EQUALS 1/2 INCH

1/4 DOWEL,
1 1/4 LONG

PART K

3/4 DOWEL, 3/4 LONG

TOP

PART J

$\frac{1}{2}$

1/4 DRILL, 3/8
DEEP, CENTERED
(NOT SHOWN)

3/4 DOWEL
1 1/2 LONG

1/4 DRILL
1/2 DEEP

PART I

TAPERED TO CENTER

American/British Terminology

American terms appear first. Their British equivalents follow in parentheses.

absorbent cotton (cotton wool)
alcohol (white spirit)
backsaw (tenon saw)
bar clamp (sash clamp)
base frame (plinth)
bench dogs (bench stops)
block joint fittings (bloc joint fittings)
bolt (burr hole)
brads (panel pins)
burlap (wall hessian)
burls (burrs)
can (tin)
carcass (carcase)
casters (castors)
C-clamp (G cramp)
clamps (cramps)
clear (cleave)
clothespins (clothes pegs)
collet (gun chuck)
dado (housing joint)
dressed (ready planed)
drive in the brads (tap the pins)
edge cross lap joint (deep halving joint)
electric cord (electric flew)
end rabbet joint (lap butt joint)
factory (works)
fibreboard (hardboard)
finishing nail (lost head nail)
flathead screw (countersink screw)
grounding (earthing)
hand drill (drill-gun)
hood (bonnet)
jointer (surfacer)

jointing (topping)
laying out (setting out)
lumber (timber)
nail set (panel pin punch)
nail the corners (pin the corners)
panels (cheeks)
plain rabbet joint (plain butt joint)
plane iron cap (curling iron)
plastic sheet (polythene)
plow plane (plough plane)
pocket cut (plunge cut)
rabbet (rebate)
rabbet plane (shoulder plane)
rubbing compound (cutting-door plaster)
sandpaper (glasspaper)
screw eye (wood screw with ringed shank)
set the brads (punch the pins)
shaped (spindled)
sliding T bevel (sliding bevel)
spade bit (flatbit)
Stanley picture frame vise (Stanley frame cramp)
steel wool (wire wool)
table saw (sawbench)
3 corner file (3 sided file)
topping (jointing)
tow truck (breakdown truck)
tracing paper (transparent paper)
trial clamp (trial cramp)
trunk (boot)
van (lorry)
vise (vice)
white shellac (white polish)

METRIC EQUIVALENCY CHART

MM—MILLIMETRES   CM—CENTIMETRES

INCHES TO MILLIMETRES AND CENTIMETRES

INCHES	MM	CM	INCHES	CM	INCHES	CM
⅛	3	0.3	9	22.9	30	76.2
¼	6	0.6	10	25.4	31	78.7
⅜	10	1.0	11	27.9	32	81.3
½	13	1.3	12	30.5	33	83.8
⅝	16	1.6	13	33.0	34	86.4
¾	19	1.9	14	35.6	35	88.9
⅞	22	2.2	15	38.1	36	91.4
1	25	2.5	16	40.6	37	94.0
1¼	32	3.2	17	43.2	38	96.5
1½	38	3.8	18	45.7	39	99.1
1¾	44	4.4	19	48.3	40	101.6
2	51	5.1	20	50.8	41	104.1
2½	64	6.4	21	53.3	42	106.7
3	76	7.6	22	55.9	43	109.2
3½	89	8.9	23	58.4	44	111.8
4	102	10.2	24	61.0	45	114.3
4½	114	11.4	25	63.5	46	116.8
5	127	12.7	26	66.0	47	119.4
6	152	15.2	27	68.6	48	121.9
7	178	17.8	28	71.1	49	124.5
8	203	20.3	29	73.7	50	127.0

YARDS TO METRES

YARDS	METRES	YARDS	METRES	YARDS	METRES	YARDS	METRES	YARDS	METRES
⅛	0.11	2⅛	1.94	4⅛	3.77	6⅛	5.60	8⅛	7.43
¼	0.23	2¼	2.06	4¼	3.89	6¼	5.72	8¼	7.54
⅜	0.34	2⅜	2.17	4⅜	4.00	6⅜	5.83	8⅜	7.66
½	0.46	2½	2.29	4½	4.11	6½	5.94	8½	7.77
⅝	0.57	2⅝	2.40	4⅝	4.23	6⅝	6.06	8⅝	7.89
¾	0.69	2¾	2.51	4¾	4.34	6¾	6.17	8¾	8.00
⅞	0.80	2⅞	2.63	4⅞	4.46	6⅞	6.29	8⅞	8.12
1	0.91	3	2.74	5	4.57	7	6.40	9	8.23
1⅛	1.03	3⅛	2.86	5⅛	4.69	7⅛	6.52	9⅛	8.34
1¼	1.14	3¼	2.97	5¼	4.80	7¼	6.63	9¼	8.46
1⅜	1.26	3⅜	3.09	5⅜	4.91	7⅜	6.74	9⅜	8.57
1½	1.37	3½	3.20	5½	5.03	7½	6.86	9½	8.69
1⅝	1.49	3⅝	3.31	5⅝	5.14	7⅝	6.97	9⅝	8.80
1¾	1.60	3¾	3.43	5¾	5.26	7¾	7.09	9¾	8.92
1⅞	1.71	3⅞	3.54	5⅞	5.37	7⅞	7.20	9⅞	9.03
2	1.83	4	3.66	6	5.49	8	7.32	10	9.14

Index

Adjustable shelves, making, 42
Adjustable triangle, 16, 17
Aircraft
    biplane, 169–175
    helicopter, 184–188
    Piper Cub, 176–183
Airplanes' fuselages, making, 43, 44
"Alphabet of lines," 11, 13
Appliance knobs, making, 42, 43
Assembly drawing, 8, 9

Band saw, 21, 22
Bayonet saw. *See* sabre saw
Belt sander, 19
Biplane, 169–175
Bow compass, 16, 17

Cars
    MG, 60–65
    Model T coupé, 66–71
    Model T sedan, 48–53
Center line, 13
Circle template, 16, 17
Crane, 91–97

Diamond nose, 32
Dimension line, 13
Disc sander, 35, 36
Dowelling jig, 42
Drill press, 27, 28

Eighteen wheeler, 72–83
Electric hand drill, 20, 21
Electric handsaw, 20
Electric jigsaw. *See* sabre saw
Extension line, 13

Faceplate turning, 32, 33
Finish sander. *See* orbital sander
Folding ruler, 16
Forstner bit, 37, 38
    for making spoke wheels, 45
Framing square, 16
French curve, 16

Games
    penny pool, 161–163
    skittles, 164–168
Gouge, 32
Grids, 14, 15

Hand drill, electric, 20, 21

Handsaw, electric, 20
Helicopter, 184–188
Hidden line, 11, 13
Hole saw, 45, 46
Household "appliances"
    ironing board and iron, 106–110
    refrigerator and freezer, 134–140
    sink, 127–133
    stove, 119–126
    toaster, 111–114
    vacuum cleaner, 115–118

Ironing board and iron, 106–110
Isometric drawing, 6, 7

Jigsaw, 26, 27
Jointer, 22, 23, 24
    rabbet cut on a, 40, 41

Marking gauge, 16
Mechanical drawings, 6–17
    depicting objects being turned, 15, 16
    lines used in, 11, 13, 14
    symbols used in, 14
    tools for laying out, 15, 16–17
    types of, 6, 7–10, 11
MG, 60–65
Model T coupé, 66–71
Model T sedan, 48–53
Mortises, cutting, 42, 43
Mortising machines, 34, 35
"Moving" vehicles
    crane, 91–97
    eighteen wheeler, 72–83
    MG, 60–65
    Model T coupé, 66–71
    Model T sedan, 48–53
    pickup truck, 54–59
    steam shovel, 84–90
    train, 98–105
Multiview drawings, 8, 10, 11, 12

Object line, 11, 13
Oblique drawing, 6, 8
Oblong cuts, inside, 39
One-point perspective, 8
Orbital sander, 19

Parting tool, 32
Penny pool, 161–163

Pickup truck, 54–59
Pictorial drawings, 6 7–9
Piper Cub, 176–183
Planer, 24, 25, 26
Plywood, cutting, 46
Puzzles
    alphabet, 148, 149–151
    brace, 156
    C-clamp, 160
    dog, 143
    duck, 145
    fish, 144
    goose, 147
    hammer, 154
    hand drill, 153
    numbers, 148, 152
    plane, 155
    saw, 159
    screwdriver, 158
    turtle, 146
    wrench, 157

Rabbet joints, 23
    cutting, 40, 41
Radial arm saw, 33, 34
Refrigerator and freezer, 134–140
Round nose, 32
Round plugs, making, 39, 40
Router, 19, 20

Sabre saw, 18, 19
Scroll saw. *See* jigsaw
Section line, 13, 14
Section view, 11, 13
Sink, 127–133
Skew, 32
Skittles, 164–168
Spindle sander, 34, 35
Spindle turning, 32
Spoke wheels, making, 45, 46
Steam shovel, 84–90

Stove, 119–126
Surfacer. *See* planer
Table saw, 28, 29–30, 31
    rabbet cut on a, 40, 41
Tape measure, 16
Templates, for isometric drawings, 6
Thickness planer. *See* planer
Three-point perspective, 8, 9
Toaster, 111–114
Tools, for layout of mechanical drawings, 15,
    16–17
Tools, power, 18–36
    band saw, 21, 22
    belt sander, 19
    disc sander, 35, 36
    drill press, 27, 28
    electric hand drill, 20, 21
    electric handsaw, 20
    jigsaw, 26, 27
    jointer, 22, 23, 24
    orbital sander, 19
    planer, 24, 25, 26
    radial arm saw, 33, 34
    router, 19, 20
    sabre saw, 18, 19
    spindle sander, 34, 35
    table saw, 28, 29–30, 31
    wood lathe, 31, 32, 33
Train, 98–105
Trammel points, 16, 17
Try square, 16
Turnings, drawings of, 15, 16
Two-point perspective, 8

Vacuum cleaner, 115–118
V-block, 37
Vertical drum sander. *See* spindle sander
Visible line. *See* object line

Wood lathe, 31, 32, 33
Working drawing, 8